Cinderella

A

Book, music and lyrics by
David Wood

Samuel French – London
New York – Sydney – Toronto – Hollywood

CINDERELLA

First produced at the Queen's Theatre, Hornchurch on the 10th December, 1979, with the following cast of characters—

King Septimus	Roger Booth
Queen Ermintrude	Penny Jones
William	Richard Barnes
Prince Charming	Rob Edwards
Bella	John Halstead
Donna	Kevin Williams
Baron Hardy	Peter Theedom
Cinderella	Pauline Siddle
Horse	{ Graham Hoadly
	{ Robert Meadwell
Fairy Godmother	Audrey Leybourne
Mouse	Yvonne Edgell
Mouse	Patience Tomlinson
Hairdresser	Graham Hoadly
Beautician	Robert Meadwell
Jester	David Brenchley

Also in the company were Lindsey Peters and Julian Freeman. The children were:

Choir A: Gillian Bailey, Fiona Barbour, Richard Drew, Lynn Fairbrass, Lisa Farrant, Mark Hobbs, Katherine Howard, Pepe Martinez, Suzanne Ross, Clare Terry

Choir B: John Barrett, Sue Butler, Jonathan Doherty, Georgina Field, Nicola Field, Karen Holmes, Larry Merry, Joanne Saunders, Beverley Smith, Jacqueline White

The play directed by Paul Tomlinson

Choreography by Lorelei Lynn

Settings by Ian Wilson

Costumes designed by Sue King

Musical Director Simon Webb

MUSICAL NUMBERS

ACT 1

1	The Christmas Fayre	Jester, Minstrels and Company
1a	Music for 'The Cinderella Story'	
2	We're Gonna Have a Ball	Prince Charming, King, Queen and Company
2a	Scene Link	
3	Not a Pretty Sight	Cinderella, Baron, Bella, Donna
3a	Play-off music	
4	At the End of the Tunnel	Cinderella, Baron
4a	Scene Link	
5	Give Us a Kiss!	Bella, Donna, Prince Charming, William
5a	Mice entrance music	
6	Squeak, Squeak, Squeak!	Cinderella, the Mice
7	Shoo!	Bella, Donna
8	Funky Monkey	Cinderella, Prince Charming and Company
8a	Shoo! (reprise)	King, Queen and Company
9	Tonight is the Night	Bella, Donna, Hairdresser, Beautician
9a	Scene Link	
9b	At the End of the Tunnel (reprise)	Fairy Godmother
9c	Tonight is the Night (reprise)	Fairy Godmother and Company

ACT II

10	The Ball (*music only*)	
11	The Ugly Tango (*music only*)	
12	The Christmas Waltz (*music only*)	
12a	The Funky Monkey (reprise)	All
12b	The Christmas Waltz (sung reprise)	All
12c	Settling down music	

13	One Glass Slipper	Cinderella, Prince Charming
14	Spread the Word	Company (except Cinderella and the Mice)
14a	Scene link	
14b	Fanfare	
15	Will the Slipper Fit?	Prince Charming, William, King, Queen, Baron, Jester and Chorus
15a	At the End of the Tunnel (reprise)	Cinderella, Baron, Prince Charming and Company
16	Happy Wedding Day/ Walkdown	Bella, Donna, Audience and Company
16a	The Funky Monkey (reprise)	All

CHARACTERS — DOUBLING SUGGESTIONS

1	(M)	KING SEPTIMUS
2	(F)	QUEEN ERMINTRUDE
3	(M)	WILLIAM
4	(M)	PRINCE CHARMING
5	(M or F)	BELLA
6	(M or F)	DONNA
7	(M)	BARON/GUEST OR STALLHOLDER AT XMAS FAYRE
8	(F)	CINDERELLA
9	(F)	FAIRY GODMOTHER/GUEST, STALLHOLDER OR MINSTREL AT XMAS FAYRE/'CHORUS' IN SONG 8/GUEST AT BALL
10	(M or F)	MOUSE 1/GUEST, STALLHOLDER OR MINSTREL AT XMAS FAYRE/'CHORUS' IN SONG 8/GUEST AT BALL
11	(F)	MOUSE 2/GUEST, STALLHOLDER OR MINSTREL AT XMAS FAYRE/'CHORUS' IN SONG 8/GUEST AT BALL
12	(M or F)	HORSE—FRONT END/GUEST, STALLHOLDER OR MINSTREL AT XMAS FAYRE/COACHMAN/HAIRDRESSER/WORKMAN/'CHORUS' IN SONG 8/GUEST AT BALL
13	(M or F)	HORSE—BACK END/GUEST, STALLHOLDER OR MINSTREL AT XMAS FAYRE/COACHMAN/BEAUTICIAN/WORKMAN/'CHORUS' IN SONG 8/GUEST AT BALL
14	(M)	JESTER/COACHMAN
	CHILDREN	to play GUESTS AT XMAS FAYRE, FROG (OPTIONAL), GNOMES (OPTIONAL), 'CHORUS' in SONG 8 and GUESTS AT THE BALL
		a child could also play the DANCING BEAR

NOTE ON THE CHARACTERS

CINDERELLA is stronger than the usual image. She has to handle solo audience participation

KING SEPTIMUS is imperious and overbearing—a "hunting, shooting and fishing" type

QUEEN ERMINTRUDE is concerned, nervous, overprotective of the Prince

WILLIAM, a courtier, is Prince Charming's friend and aide; pleasant and obliging

PRINCE CHARMING is, in a way, the "ugly duckling" of this version: in other words, he is *not* the traditional, handsome Prince Charming. He only blossoms in the presence of, and because of the kindness of, Cinderella

BELLA and DONNA are fairly traditional Ugly Sisters, but are horribly real in their selfish and callous behaviour

BARON HARDY, their stepfather and Cinderella's *real* father, is a dithery, frightened rabbit of a man

FAIRY GODMOTHER is amusingly down-to-earth rather than balletic

TWO MICE: they are mute (except for squeaks) and the hero and heroine of the show—lovable, cheeky and nimble

JESTER is omnipresent in the Court scenes—verbally and acrobatically clever

THE HORSE is stubborn yet spirited

For the GNOMES (optional) as many children as possible should be used. In the Christmas Fayre scene (Act I, Scene 1), as many people as possible should be on stage as stallholders, visitors, minstrels, etc. The children also should be present in this scene, as well as the Ball scene, the "Funky Monkey" (Song 8), the slipper-fitting scene and the wedding celebration song.

ACT I

The Courtyard of the Palace—The Christmas Fayre. Evening, a week before Christmas

All the traditional Christmas Fayre stalls and activities are here—hot chestnuts over a brazier, an ox roasting, a toffee-apple stall, hot toddies, "Knock Off the Snowman's Hat", Hoopla, using deer antlers, bran tub, a fortune-teller, perhaps a dancing bear. There is a crisp, snowy feeling, plus a large Christmas tree

Guests, Stallholders and Children take part. The Jester juggles or tumbles. Possibly a small group of Minstrels or Travelling Players perform with tabors, drums, tambourine, handbells, leading the singing

As the CURTAIN rises after a short overture, the Fayre is "frozen", the Jester downstage

SONG 1: **The Christmas Fayre**

Jester
'Tis the time, 'tis the season
Of mistletoe and holly berry
The rhyme and the reason
For letting go and making merry
Hey derry
Ho derry
Roll up and share
All the fun of the Christmas Fayre.

The Fayre bursts into life and Lights brighten

All
'Tis the time, 'tis the season
Of mistletoe and holly berry
The rhyme and the reason
For letting go and making merry
Hey derry
Ho derry
Roll up and share
All the fun of the Christmas Fayre.

Singers singing
Bell-ringers ringing
Drummers drumming
Christmas is coming.

MUSICAL BRIDGE (the first four lines of chorus) during which GUESTS mingle, etc.

Hey derry
Ho derry
Dance with a bear

The Dancing Bear is featured

And have fun at the Christmas Fayre

The music continues

The King and Queen enter regally, waving

Their Subjects bow low

The Royal Couple is led in by William, a Courtier, who is also the Prince's friend and bodyguard

They reach a dais and climb up. The King looks around, anxious, as they sit on their thrones. A third throne is empty

King (*sotto voce*) Where is he?
William Your Majesty?
King The Prince. Where is he?
William I don't know, Your Majesty.
King What do you mean, "I don't know, Your Majesty"? You're his friend and bodyguard, aren't you? How can you guard a body if you don't know where it is?
William I'll go and look for him, Your Majesty.
Queen Be gentle with him, William, he's such a nervy little boy. He's never liked crowds.
King For heaven's sake, Ermintrude, our nervy little boy is nineteen years old. (*He waves William away*)

William goes off

SONG 1 **The Christmas Fayre** (Part 2)

All   'Tis the time, 'tis the season
Of mistletoe and holly berry
The rhyme and the reason
For letting go and making merry
Hey derry
Ho derry
Let down your hair
Join the fun of the Christmas Fayre.

Sideshows, prizes
Funny disguises

One or two people are featured wearing funny masks

Try your skill, now
Come eat your fill, now

A Trader, with a box of toffee apples is featured

All   'Tis the time, 'tis the season
                  Of mistletoe and holly berry
                  The rhyme and the reason
                  For letting go and making merry
                  Hey derry
                  Ho derry
                  Let down your hair
                  Hey derry
                  Ho derry
                  Dance with a bear
                  Hey derry
                  Ho derry
                  Roll up and share
                  All the fun of the Christmas Fayre.

At the end of the song, William returns

Meanwhile, the Stallholders and Guests look at the royal dais expectantly

William Still no sign, Your Majesty.
King Oh, suffering sceptres, I'll have to do it myself. Scroll.

William hands him a scroll from a small table. The King unrolls it

The Royal glasses.

William hands him a tray of goblets

No, no, you fool, the Royal *reading* glasses.
William Sorry, Your Majesty.

William finds an ornate pair of spectacles or a lorgnette. He hands them to the King, who has to let go of one end of the scroll to receive them. The scroll rolls up again. The King "tut-tuts", and eventually gets William to hold the unrolled scroll, while he reads

King   Christmas is coming
                  There's joy everywhere
                  So what could be better
                  Than a Christmas Fayre?
                  Who wrote this rubbish?
Queen You did, dear.
King Oh. Did I? Mm. (*He continues*)
                  And now is the moment
                  When the Christmas Fayre
                  Is officially open,
                  I declare. (*He raises his eyes heavenward at the dire verse*)

Applause. The King presses a button and the Christmas Tree lights up. "Ooohs" and "Aaahs" and more applause. The Stallholders and Guests return to their activities

Right, that's it. Come on, Ermintrude.

Queen We can't go in yet dear. We have to do something. It's expected.

King Do something? Do what?

Queen (*making a suggestion*) Knock a snowman's hat off.

King Seems a particularly stupid thing to do.

Queen It's fun, dear.

King Not much fun for the snowman. (*He laughs heartily*)

Queen (*walking towards a stall*) Well, let's have a lucky dip in the bran tub.

King Oh, very well.

Stallholder Stick your hand in! Prize every time!

Queen The Royal Purse, William.

William pays the Stallholder

Stallholder Thank you, Your Majesties. Rummage away.

The King puts his hand in the bran tub, which is full of coloured paper, streamers, etc. After a quick rummage, he looks bemused, then pulls out the Prince, looking sheepish, carrying a book. He wears royal glasses, too

King What on earth . . .?

Queen Charming! You naughty boy. What are you doing in there?

Prince Charming Sorry, Mother, I was reading and I fell asleep.

Queen Oh, Charming! Baby! (*She embraces him*)

King Leave him alone. Don't mollycoddle him. (*He drags him downstage out of earshot*)

The Queen and William follow

Now, look here, Charming—and that's another thing, Ermintrude, how I ever agreed to your calling him Charming I'll never know. Of all the stupid names.

Queen It's not. It's a—

King $\left.\begin{array}{l}\text{\textbf{King}} \\ \text{\textbf{Queen}}\end{array}\right\}$ charming name— $\left\{\begin{array}{l}\textit{Speaking} \\ \textit{together}\end{array}\right.$

King —yes, now listen, Charming, you were meant to open this Fayre. I wrote you a special Fayre-declaring-open poem.

Prince Charming I'm sorry, Father. I couldn't face it.

King Face it! You wander around the palace with a face as long as a ferret. You never do any normal things like elephant-hunting or channel swimming. Why don't you just perk up a bit, eh?

Queen It's just a phase. (*To Prince Charming*) Isn't it, dear?

King Phase? More like a daze. He hasn't laughed for about three years. (*Calling*) Jester!

The Jester runs forward

Jester Your Majesty?

King Make the Prince laugh.

Jester Make the Prince laugh? You must be joking.

King No. *You* must be joking. Joking's your job. Jesters jest, don't they?

Jester Yes, but—the Prince? Oh, all right, here goes. Special Christmas joke. Why does Father Christmas wear a red mac?

King (*entering into the spirit*) I don't know. Why *does* Father Christmas wear a red mac?

Jester Because of the reindeer—get it? Rain, dear!

The King roars with laughter. The Prince does not react at all. The King laughing all the time, looks over to the Prince, encouraging him to laugh. No success. After a bit, the King stops laughing abruptly

King Mm, well it wasn't all that funny, I must admit.

The King glares at the Jester, who shrugs and steps back

Prince Charming (*smiling*) Father, it's nothing to do with laughing or elephant hunting or channel swimming. I'm just fed up. Bored with being a Prince. I just want to be a normal person.

King But you're not a normal person. (*Shouting*) That's the whole point. Princes can't be normal.

Queen Don't shout, dear. Of course Charming is normal, just a little sensitive and highly strung. What he needs is to meet more people, more more-or-less normal people. Of his own age.

Prince Charming Mother, I don't.

Queen Hush, Charming, Mummy knows best. Doesn't she, Daddy?

King (*raising his eyes heavenward*) What are you suggesting, Ermintrude?

Queen We'll have a splendid party, a ball (*Idea*) a fancy dress ball, on Christmas Eve, and invite lots of *normal* people. William, the Royal pen and paper.

William Yes, Your Majesty. (*He finds them*)

King Mm. Good thinking, Ermintrude.

Queen Thank you, dear.

Prince Charming But Mother, I can't dance.

Queen You'll have to learn, darling.

Prince Charming And I'm not wearing fancy dress.

Queen Now then, let's think of some nice *normal* people. The Duke and Duchess of Hartingdon and daughter—

William takes notes

Viscount Willoughby, Lord and Lady Lexingfold and their son and daughter. Who else?

King That Baron, er, you know, behaves like a frightened rabbit—Hardy, that's it—Baron Hardy—and his two daughters.

Queen Of course.

William Three, Your Majesty.

King Mm?

Queen Three what, William?

William Three daughters, Your Majesty. Baron Hardy has three daughters.

King Utter rot and balderdash, William. I've met them. There are only two. Bella and Donna.

William I beg your pardon, Your Majesty, three. Bella, Donna and—Cinderella.

MUSIC 1A

The lighting changes as we go into a stylized version of the story of Baron Hardy's Daughters. This can be mimed out by Children, or acted out in silhouette, or even by puppets, in the form of a puppet show at the Fayre. At the Director's discretion it can be done "straight", or, if it suits the style, for laughs. For example, when the Stepmother dies, it could be mimed seriously or she could do a slapstick throat-clutching death. Another possibility is that we should actually see the real characters at this point—as it were, through a hazy gauze—miming their own lives. But this may be felt to pre-empt the appearance of those characters in the next scene. In the original production a stylized mime using masks proved very effective. Whatever is decided upon, William tells the story and it is enacted before us. Other Guests and Stallholders become the audience

William You see, Baron Hardy, Your Majesty, didn't always behave like a frightened rabbit. He was once a man of strong character. He married the haughty Lady Belladonna. She had two daughters by her first marriage—Bella and Donna—who were exactly like their mother in all ways. The Baron had also been married before, to the kindest, gentlest of ladies, who sadly died shortly after the birth of their daughter—Cinderella. As she grew up, Cinderella became exactly like her mother. But no sooner was the Lady Belladonna married to the Baron than her true character showed itself. She treated the Baron far worse than a servant, and because Cinderella was prettier than her own daughters, she treated her cruelly like a slave. She made her do all the housework and cooking, while Bella and Donna did nothing. And while Bella and Donna slept in comfortable beds upstairs, Cinderella was forced to sleep in the kitchen. Then Lady Balladonna died. And the Baron thought things would get better. But they didn't, and Bella and Donna continue to rule the household like their mother, and still treat Cinderella like a slave. She's never allowed out except to run errands and do the shopping, and very few people even know she exists. The Baron desperately wants to help Cinderella, but he's so frightened of his two step-daughters that he allows them to do as they please. And Cinderella is such a good-natured girl that for the sake of her father she never complains.

The Mime ends. The Lighting returns to normal

So you see, Your Majesty, Baron Hardy has three daughters, not two.

The Guests and Stallholders return to their places. There is a short pause as the story sinks in

Queen That poor child.
Prince Charming (*suddenly*) She must be invited.
King What?
Prince Charming To the Fancy Dress Ball. She must come. It's the least we can do to help her.
King Impossible. William said she's never allowed out.
Queen Probably has nothing suitable to wear.

Prince Charming Well, that doesn't matter. It's fancy dress. She can come in anything. I insist she's sent an invitation.

William She'll probably never even be allowed to open the envelope, Your Highness.

Prince Charming (*full of enthusiasm*) Then I shall deliver it to her myself. Come on, William, let's do the invitations. Take this down, please . . .

The King and Queen are naturally happy that at last he seems to be interested in something

SONG 2: **We're Gonna Have a Ball**

During the song, the Company should possibly come downstage, in front of a frontcloth, in order to facilitate the scene change into Scene 2, or if the Baron's Kitchen is trucked in sections, a visual scene change at the end of the song could be interesting

Prince Charming (*dictating, as it were*)

> His Majesty King Septimus
> Her Majesty Queen Ermintrude
> And his Highness Prince Charming
> Take pleasure in inviting you all
> To a fabulous, marvellous,
> Christmas fancy dress ball.

During the invitations everyone shows interest and the excitement as the news ripples through the crowd

King
Queen   } We're gonna have a ball
Prince Charming It'll be a grand affair
Ev'ryone who's anyone
Is gonna to be going there.

All (*Except   We're gonna have a ball
The Royal   Ev'ryone in fancy dress
Family*)   When the invitations come
We're gonna say "yes".

We're gonna have a ball
It'll be a grand affair
Ev'ryone who's anyone
Is gonna be going there.

We're gonna have a ball
It's a time to celebrate
When the invitations come
We're gonna say 'great'.

The twenty fourth of December
Will be
A night to remember
You'll see.

The Royal Family and William hand out invitations

King	
Queen	}
Prince Charming	

We're gonna have a ball
It'll be a grand affair
Ev'ryone who's anyone
Is gonna be going there.

We're gonna have a ball
It'll be a wild success

All (*Except*
The Royal
Family)

When the invitations come
We're gonna say "yes".

The Prince watches as the others waltz

All

We'll dance and we'll dance and we'll dance
Our feet hardly touching the floor
We'll dance and we'll dance
And if we get the chance
We'll dance and we'll dance some more.

We're gonna have a ball
It'll be a grand affair
Ev'ryone who's anyone
Is gonna be going there

We're gonna have a ball
Ev'ryone in fancy dress
When the invitations come
We're gonna say "yes".

All read out their invitations

His Majesty King Septimus
Her Majesty Queen Ermintrude
And his Highness Prince Charming
Take pleasure in inviting you all
To a fabulous, marvellous,
Splendid, opulent,
Christmas fancy dress ball.

King	
Queen	} R.S.V.P.
Prince Charming	

MUSIC 2A

SCENE 2

The Baron's Kitchen

*There is the traditional large open fireplace, with glowing fire and a kettle on
the hob; a stove; a dresser against one wall, with pots and pans and plates; a*

kitchen table with chairs; a sink; an ironing-board; a cupboard set square on to the audience. On the dresser or elsewhere are various foodstuffs, vegetables, etc. A door at the back leads outside, and another to other rooms

Cinderella enters through the back door, carrying a large basket of laundry she has just collected off the washing line. There is nothing resentful about her, and nothing stoic. She is simply doing a job. She takes a sheet or pillowcase out and puts it on the ironing board. She collects a hot iron from the hob and starts to press a light-coloured scarf. All the while she hums a tune—possibly "Not a Pretty Sight".

Suddenly there is a tentative knocking sound. Cinderella reacts to it. It stops. She continues ironing. Another few taps. She reacts again, and, leaving the iron upended, she goes to investigate. The tapping leads her to the cupboard. She calls through the door, a bit cautious.

Cinderella Who's there?
Voice (*from inside the cupboard*) Who's there?
Cinderella Who are you?
Voice Who are *you*?
Cinderella I asked first. Who are you?
Voice Cinderella . . .?
Cinderella *I'm* Cinderella.
Voice That's all right, then.

Cinderella will stand no nonsense any more. She unlocks the door and pulls it open

Baron Hardy is seated uncomfortably on a shelf several feet from the ground

Cinderella Father. What are you doing in there?
Baron Trying to get out, dear.
Cinderella But how did you get in in the first place?
Baron Your stepsisters locked me in here, dear.
Cinderella Why?
Baron Because I haven't managed to find them husbands yet. They wanted to show me what it was like being on the shelf.
Cinderella Oh, Father. Come on down.

She helps him down. He is bent double

How could they be so rotten? (*She returns to her ironing*)
Baron In a word, dear, easily. (*He straightens painfully*) Oh, if only I could marry them off and be rid of them for ever. But any self-respecting young man wouldn't give either of them a second look; probably wouldn't give either of them a *first* look. (*Raising his voice*) They're so *ugly*. (*He stops, and listens nervously*) What was that?
Cinderella What?
Baron They're coming. They're coming. Put me back in the cupboard. They'll go mad if they think I've escaped. Quick. (*He scrabbles at the cupboard*)

Cinderella It's all right, Father. You're hearing things. You mustn't let Bella and Donna frighten you.
Baron They don't frighten me. They terrify me! And the way they treat you, dear, it's disgraceful. It's—not fair. It's—going to stop. (*He looks resolute*) It's—
Donna (*off, calling from outside the back door*) Cinderella!
Baron —time I was off! (*He scuttles to the inner door—but stops in his tracks when he hears Bella call*)
Bella (*off, from outside inner door*) Cinderella! (*He changes direction back towards the back door, and reaches it as it opens; he is forced to hide behind it—between it and the wall—as the door opens*)

Donna stands in the doorway

Donna Cinderella.
Cinderella Yes, Donna.
Donna Have you scrubbed this floor today?
Cinderella Yes, Donna.
Donna What a pity! (*Entering with muddy, snowy shoes or boots and deliberately trampling it over the floor*) My boots are filthy. You'll have to scrub it all over again, won't you?
Cinderella Yes, Donna.
Donna Now!

Cinderella leaves the ironing, gets a bucket with soap and a scrubbing brush and starts work. Donna walks smugly towards the inner door, smiling snootily at the audience

Bella (*calling from outside the inner door*) Cinderella!

The door opens, smashing into Donna, and Bella enters

Cinderella Yes, Bella.
Bella What are you doing on the floor? This is no time for resting. Get up.
Cinderella (*standing*) But I'm scrubbing . . .
Bella And don't answer back. Do some work, you lazy layabout. There must be plenty to do. (*Looking round*) This floor looks filthy for a start. Scrub it.
Cinderella But that's what I . . .
Bella Scrub it.
Cinderella Yes, Bella. (*She starts work again*)
Bella Where's Donna?
Donna (*emerging, rubbing her nose*) Here, dear.
Bella Where have you been?
Donna Outside looking for you.
Bella I was inside.
Donna I know you were inside.
Bella If you knew I was inside, why were you looking outside?
Donna I didn't know you were inside till I'd been outside and found you weren't there.
Bella Where?
Donna Outside.

Bella I wasn't outside, I was inside.
Donna I know you were inside *now*, but I didn't know you were inside *then*.
Bella When?
Donna When I was outside.
Bella (*after a pause*) You've lost me.
Donna Exactly. That's why I went outside. To find you. But you weren't there. So I came inside. And you were.
Bella Well, now you *have* found me, what do you want?
Donna I've forgotten.
Bella Ooh, you big silly cissie sister. (*She shudders*) There's a terrible draught in here. Cinderella.
Cinderella Yes, Bella.
Bella Shut that door.
Cinderella (*knowing her father is behind it*) But . . .
Bella Don't argue. Shut it.
Cinderella Yes, Bella.

Cinderella gets up and shuts the door, revealing the terrified Baron. Bella does huge double-take

Bella Oh look!
Donna It's Stepdaddy!
Bella ⎫
Donna ⎬ Hello, Stepdaddy!   { *Speaking together*
Baron Hello, girls. (*He waves nervously*)

They go to him and carry him upright downstage

Donna How did Stepdaddy get out of the cupboard, Bella?
Bella I think our little goody goody sickly sweet stepsister Cinderella let him out. Didn't she?
Baron N-no, dear . . .
Donna ⎫
Bella ⎬ (*to the audience*) Oh, yes she did.   { *Speaking together*
Audience Oh, no she didn't.
Donna ⎫
Bella ⎬ Oh, yes she did.   { *Speaking together*
Audience Oh, no she didn't.
Donna ⎫
Bella ⎬ Did.   { *Speaking together*
Audience Didn't.
Donna ⎫
Bella ⎬ Did. Did. Did.   { *Speaking together*
Audience Didn't. Didn't. Didn't.
Bella Anyway, we're glad you're here, Stepdaddy.
Baron Really, girls?
Donna Ever so glad.
Baron Thank you. Why?
Donna Why, Bella?
Bella Because we're going to buy our Christmas presents today.

Baron Oh, how kind, girls. What are you buying me?

Donna You're not listening, Stepdaddy.

Bella We're going to buy *our* Christmas presents. For *you* to give *us*.

Baron Oh. Yes. Very thoughtful of you.

Donna So we'll need a little bit of pocket-money, Stepdaddy, dear.

Baron But, girls, I've given you so many little bits of pocket-money
 recently.

Bella But how can you resistywist two such beautiweautiful girliwirlies?
 Mmm?

*They edge in, eyes closed, to kiss him. He backs away, revolted, at the last
moment, and the Uglies kiss each other*

Bella } Ugh! { *Speaking*
Donna }   { *together*

They grab the Baron in a half-nelson

Bella Money, Stepdaddy.

Baron Girls, please. There's hardly any more money left. In the village they
 don't call me Baron Hardy any more. They call me Baron Hardup.

Donna Where's your piggy bank, Stepdaddy?

Baron Oh no, not my piggy bank, please. I'm saving up.

Bella What for?

The Baron shakes his head; the Uglies increase the half-nelson.

Baron A new dress for Cinderella.

*There is a gasping pause from the Uglies as this sinks in. Cinderella comes
downstage at the mention of her name*

Bella A—

Donna —new—

Bella —dress—

Donna —for—

Bella } Cinderella? { *Speaking*
Donna }   { *together*

The Baron nods

Bella How dare you! She doesn't need a new dress. She's ugly and horrid
 and ugh!

Donna We're oodles more beautiful than her. (*To the audience*) Aren't we?

Audience No.

Bella } Oh, yes we are. { *Speaking*
Donna }   { *together*

Audience Oh, no you're not.

Bella } Oh yes we are. { *Speaking*
Donna }   { *together*

Audience Oh, no you're not.

Bella } Are. { *Speaking*
Donna }   { *together*

Audience Aren't.

The attention of the Uglies is diverted as Cinderella walks resolutely to the fireplace

Bella (*sharply*) Where are you going?
Cinderella To get Father's piggy bank for you.

The Uglies drop the Baron in surprise

Donna It's in the fireplace!

They rush towards it

Bella Out of the way.
Cinderella It's dirty; *I'll* . . .
Bella OUT OF THE WAY!

Cinderella stands aside. The Uglies both go towards the fireplace and bump into each other

Donna After you, Bella dear.
Bella After you, Donna dear.
Donna ⎫
              Thank you.   ⎧ *Speaking*
Bella ⎭   ⎩ *together*

Both go together and bump into each other again

Aaaaah!
Bella *You* get it, Donna.

Donna goes into the fireplace and searches

Have you washed and ironed my silk scarf, Cinderella?
Cinderella Yes, Bella.

Cinderella hands the scarf to Bella, as Donna is heard coughing and spluttering in the fireplace. She emerges carrying the piggy bank—and with a sooty face and hands. She puts down the piggy bank

Donna (*grabbing Bella's scarf to wipe herself*) Ugh. I'm filthy. You wicked
   girl, why didn't you tell me it was dirty? (*She hands back the filthy scarf
   and makes for Cinderella*)
Cinderella I did . . .
Donna Don't lie. Come here. I'll teach you to lie. I'll slap your hand. (*She
   starts to chase Cinderella*)
Bella That's right, dear, slap her hand. (*She goes to put on her scarf and sees
   it is filthy*) Ugh. *This* is filthy. You wicked girl, you never washed it at all.
Cinderella I did . . .
Bella Don't lie. Come here. I'll teach you to lie. I'll slap your *other* hand.

Music, as the Uglies get Cinderella between them and grab her hands. As they slap with their other hands, Cinderella manages to free herself, and the Uglies slap each other. A short chase develops. Eventually Donna slips on the soap, left by Cinderella on the floor. Bella goes to help her up but gets her own foot stuck in Cinderella's bucket. Donna gets up and tries to pull the bucket off Bella's foot. She does so, but falls backwards into Cinderella's laundry basket.

Bella tries to help Donna out, and both fall over the ironing-board. Meanwhile Cinderella and the Baron huddle together to watch.

NB: The slapstick sequence could be expanded if required; but using the basic idea of each ugly sister trying to help the other out of a situation, and ending up in a worse situation herself

The Uglies recover themselves and pounce on the piggy bank, trying to get the money out. Cinderella and the Baron come forward and watch them grovel

SONG 3: **Not a Pretty Sight**

Baron   Look at them, just look at them—
              A vision of delight!
              Scrabbling at my money box
              Like a pair of fighting cocks
              It's not a pretty sight.

Baron ⎫   Not a pretty sight
Cinderella ⎰ To tell the honest truth
              They're lazy, rude and ruthless
              Unpleasant and uncouth
              They never say please or thank you
              They tease and jeer and scoff
              They never lift a finger
              Except to tick us off.

              Not a pretty sight
              They're nasty, horrid, mean
              They're plain, in fact plain ugly
              Disgusting and obscene
              They ought to be used as scarecrows
              The birds would die of fright
              It has to be admitted
              They're not a pretty sight.

Bella and Donna finish filching from the piggy bank. Bella overhears the last line. The music continues

Bella What did you say?
Baron Er . . .
Cinderella "What a pretty sight". You and Donna.
Baron Oh yes. What a pretty sight!
Bella Mmm. We're off now. Donna, where's Cinderella's list of jobs?
Donna Here, dear.

Donna unrolls a very long scroll. Together, the Uglies issue their orders:

Bella ⎫   Dig the garden
Donna ⎰   Sweep the chimney
              Dust the ceiling
              Chop the wood

>   Make the beds and
>   Do the laundry
>   Stir the Christmas pud.

The music continues

Cinderella Is that all?
Donna No. Then you make the lunch.
Bella And *after* lunch . . .
Bella ⎫   Scrub the dustbin
Donna ⎭   Wash the curtains
>   Mend the fence, then
>   Cook our tea
>   Peel the onions
>   Clean the oven
>   Decorate the tree.

They indicate the Christmas Tree

All four sing in counterpoint

Baron ⎫	Not a pretty sight	**Donna** ⎫	Dig the garden
Cinderella ⎭	To tell the honest truth	**Bella** ⎭	Sweep the chimney
	They're lazy, rude and		Dust the ceiling
	ruthless		Chop the wood
	Unpleasant and		Make the beds and
	uncouth		Do the laundry
	They never say please		Stir the Christmas pud
	or thankyou		
	They tease and jeer		
	and scoff		
	They never lift a finger		
	Except to tick us off.		
	Not a pretty sight		Scrub the dustbin
	They're nasty, horrid,		Wash the curtains
	mean		Mend the fence, then
	They're plain, in fact		Cook our tea
	plain ugly		Peel the onions
	Disgusting and obscene		Clean the oven
	They ought to be used		Decorate the tree
	as scarecrows		
	The birds would die of		
	fright		
	It has to be admitted		
	They're not a pretty		
	sight.		

Bella ⎫ Eh? ⎧ *Speaking*
Donna ⎭   ⎩ *together*

Baron	What a pretty sight!		
Cinderella	What a pretty sight		
	Not a pretty sight!	**Bella**	Dig the garden
	Not a pretty sight	**Donna**	Sweep the chimney
	They're not a pretty		Dust the ceiling
	sight		Chop the wood
			Decorate the tree.

At the end of the song, the Music (3a) continues as the Ugly Sisters sweep out of the kitchen door—Donna holds the door open for Bella, who makes rude faces at Cinderella, the Baron and the audience, then exits. She shuts the door as Donna steps forward and makes rude faces at everyone—then goes to exit, but bangs into the closed door; she opens it and makes an undignified exit

Cinderella and the Baron are left

Cinderella Safe now, Father. (*She starts clearing up the debris*)
Baron Thank you, dear.
Cinderella Sorry I gave them the piggy bank.
Baron Well, money's not everything, is it?
Cinderella And it *has* got rid of them for a while. Sorry, anyway.
Baron Oh, Cinderella, I wish you wouldn't keep saying sorry. It's me who should be saying sorry. To you.
Cinderella Why?
Baron For letting them bully you.
Cinderella I'm sorry.
Baron There you go again. What for?
Cinderella For saying sorry.

They smile, then embrace

At least I've got you.
Baron Fat lot of good I am.

SONG 4: **At the End of the Tunnel**

Cinderella   It isn't any help to sit and cry
Feeling sorry for yourself and asking why
But I believe there's more to life in every way
And I tell myself each and every day

Never lose sight
Of the speck of light
At the end of the tunnel
It's burning bright
Never lose faith
Never give up hope
At the end of the tunnel
You'll be all right.

The music continues under the dialogue

(*Speaking*) But the light at the end of the tunnel is sometimes a bit faint.

Baron Your dreams *will* come true, dear. One day.

Cinderella Maybe.

Baron You mustn't give up hope, you know.

Cinderella No. I suppose not.

Baron I've never told you before, but—well, I knew you'd think I was even more stupid and soppy than I am—but when you were christened, Cinderella, one of your Godmothers was a Fairy.

Cinderella (*laughing*) Oh, Father, you can't expect me to believe that. There are no such things as fairies.

Baron I knew you'd laugh, dear. But it's true, mark my words, and she promised to look after you.

Cinderella (*not believing him*) Pull the other one. It's got fairy bells on!

Baron I'm serious, Cinderella. You *mustn't* give up hope. You must believe. Make your poor old father happy, eh?

Cinderella (*nodding*) All right.

SONG 4: (*continued*)

Baron   ⎫   Never lose sight
Cinderella ⎬   Of the speck of light
                      At the end of the tunnel
                      It's burning bright
                      Never lose faith
                      Never give up hope
                      At the end of the tunnel
                      You'll be all right.

Baron   Believe in your dreams
                      Whatever you do
                      Believe in your dreams
                      And they'll all come true.

Baron   ⎫   Never lose sight
Cinderella ⎬   Of the speck of light
                      At the end of the tunnel
                      It's burning bright
                      Never lose faith
                      Never give up hope
                      At the end of the tunnel
                      You'll be all right
                      You'll be all right
                      At the end of the tunnel
                      You'll be all right.

Scene 3

A Path through the forest

This, a front-cloth scene, is a snowy, tree-lined path that runs between the Baron's home and the Palace and Town

Music (4a) is heard as Donna enters, pulling a looped rope/reins, dragging a sledge on which sits or stands, smugly, a pantomime Horse. Bella brings up the rear, pushing the sledge. They come to a breathless halt

Bella You know, when I said "let's take the horse into town", this wasn't what I had in mind.
Donna (*breathing heavily*) Ooooh, I've got colly-wobbles!
Bella What makes you think that?
Donna My collies have gone all wobbly, look.
Bella (*to the horse*) Hey. You. Greased Lightning. Shift your chassie. (*She pushes him*)

The Horse takes no notice, but starts nibbling Donna's straw hat

"Oh what fun it is to ride on a one-horse open sleigh". (*Sarcastically*) Oh what fun. You've had your fun. It's our turn.

She sees the Horse nibbling Donna's hat

Ha, ha, ha!
Donna What are you laughing at?
Bella (*roaring*) He's stuffing himself with your straw hat.
Donna No, he's not.
Bella (*hysterically*) Yes, he is.
Donna No, he's not. I couldn't find mine this morning. I put yours on.

Bella stops laughing

Bella You stop nibbling, you nasty nag. Budge. (*She rushes to save her hat, then stops*) Hey, maybe that's the answer. Something to nibble. (*She takes out a carrot and hands it to Donna*) Try that.
Donna Eh?
Bella A carrot. Try that.

Donna looks confused, then bites the carrot and chews

Donna Very tasty.
Bella No, no. Try it on Greased Lightning.

Donna offers the Horse the carrot. He bites and chews

Donna Mm. He thinks it's tasty too.
Bella No. Oh, give it here.

She dangles it near the Horse's nose and lures him off the sledge

Good boy, good boy. Juicy carrot, juicy carrot. Come on. Come on, Lightning. Good horsey-worsey.

The Horse reaches the right position

Right. Reins, quick.

They both rush back to the sledge to get the reins. As they do so, following the scent of the carrot, the Horse turns round, so it is facing the wrong way. The Uglies don't notice this, but find the reins. Donna pulls them back over where the Horse's head should be, meanwhile Bella prepares to get on the sledge. Donna pulls the reins under the Horse's tail, then realizes something's wrong

Donna (*calling*) Lightning. Lightning! (*She pulls up his tail, searching*)
Bella What is it now, Donna?
Donna I've lost his head, Bella. It was here a moment ago.
Bella Don't be stupid. (*She gets on the sledge*) Lost his head—you've lost *your* head, more like ... (*She suddenly sees the Horse's head staring at her*) Aaaaah!

The scream frightens the Horse, who kicks with a back leg, sending Donna flying

Donna Aaaaaaaaah! (*She starts to get up*)

The horse kicks again

(*She falls over*) Aaaaah!

The Horse curtsies or puts its foot on Donna in triumph. Bella rushes round to help her up and pull her clear

Bella Speak to me, sister dear.
Donna I think I'm a gonna.
Bella A gonna, Donna?
Donna A gonna, Donna.

Bella hauls Donna to her feet

Bella Come on. Give me a leg up.

They position themselves at the Horse's side, and Bella prepares to climb aboard by placing one foot in Donna's cupped hands. As she is about to jump, the Horse circles on the spot, making Bella hop round in pursuit. Eventually she goes up, helped by Donna, but can't stop on "the saddle" and falls off the other side. The Horse turns again, knocking Donna over. Both scramble on the ground in as undignified a manner as possible; in a tangle of arms and legs

William enters, leading Prince Charming. They enter from the side opposite—on their way to the Baron's to deliver the invitations

You horrid horse, vicious beast, I'll slaughter him, etc.

As they struggle to rise, Donna sees William and the Prince staring. She first sees them from between her legs or in a likewise embarrassing position

Donna Psst. Bella. Shh ...
Bella Four-legged fiend, I'll get him ... (*Furiously*) What is it, Donna?
Donna Fellas, Bella.

Bella Oh, shut up. I'm not in the mood for . . . (*She stops short, seeing them*)
  Oooh!
Donna ⎤ *(coyly, still in awkward positions)* Coo-ee! Yoo-hoo! ⎰ *Speaking*
Bella ⎦   ⎱ *together*

William and Prince Charming cannot stop themselves snorting with laughter.
The Prince holds back a little

Donna Stop your sniggers.
Bella Avert your giggling gaze.
William I beg your pardon?
Donna Stop gawping. Haven't you ever stumbled across two lovely ladies-
  in-distress like us before?
William I've never stumbled across *anything* like you two before. (*Aside to*
  Prince Charming) Thank goodness.
Bella (*overhearing*) What?
William Thank goodness—we arrived in time to give you a hand.

William helps the Uglies up. They arrange themselves

Bella Cheek. Who do you think you are anyway?
William Ladies, kindly make way for Prince Charming.

Immediately the Uglies change gear and prostrate themselves before William

Bella ⎤ Oh, the Prince! The Prince!   ⎰ *Speaking*
Donna ⎦ Forgive us, your Principality, etc. ⎱ *together*
Donna God save our gorgeous Prince.
Bella Gracious.
Donna What!
Bella God save our *gracious* Prince
Donna Gracious no! He looks gorgeous to me.
Bella ⎤ Oh, Princey, Your Majesty, your gorgeousness, etc. ⎰ *Speaking*
Donna ⎦   ⎱ *together*
William Ladies, *this* is Prince Charming. (*He indicates*) My name's William.

Bella and Donna are still on their knees

Donna Well, why didn't you say so?
Bella Silly Billy.
Donna ⎤ (*Hobbling on their knees to Prince Charming*) ⎰ *Speaking*
Bella ⎬ Oh, Princey; your humble servant; your   ⎱ *together*
       ⎦ Principality; what a charmer, etc.
Prince Charming (*embarrassed*) Ladies, *please*—is this the way to Baron
  Hardy's residence?
Donna Yes. He's our stepdaddy.
Prince Charming (*realizing*) Oh, so you must be . . .
Bella Bella.
Donna Donna.
Prince Charming I've heard of you two.
Bella Flatterer.
Donna Butterer-upper!

Prince Charming (*ignoring their obsequious fawning*) You may have saved me a journey. I was delivering your invitations to our Fancy Dress Ball.

The Uglies are genuinely thrilled

Bella At the Palace?

Prince Charming nods

Donna Oh, your Princeyness, thank you.
Bella Thank you.
Prince Charming (*receiving the invitations from William and handing them over*) Bella. Donna. One for your stepfather.

Donna } Thank you. { *Speaking*
Bella }   { *together*

Prince Charming (*not handing it over*) And one for Cinderella.
Donna (*astounded*) Cinderella? She won't . . .

She is interrupted by Bella nudging her sharply

Bella Who, Your Highlimost?
Prince Charming Cinderella. I understand you have a stepsister called Cinderella.
Bella Oh, no we don't.
William (*coming forward*) Oh, yes you do.

Bella }
Donna } Oh, no we don't. { *Speaking*
         }   { *together*

William }
Audience } Oh, yes you do. { *Speaking*
           }   { *together*

Bella }
Donna } (*together*) We don't, don't, don't. { *Speaking*
         }   { *together*

William }
Audience } You do, do, do. { *Speaking*
           }   { *together*

Prince Charming Well, it's not worth arguing, ladies. Come on, William, we'll go and ask the Baron.

William and the Prince start to go

Bella Wait! (*Laughing with coy, calculated embarrassment*) Did you say "Cinderella"?
Prince Charming Several times.
Bella Yes, well, we do know her—a little.
Donna (*confused by Bella's tactics*) We know her very well. She's a lazy . . .
Bella Shut up, Donna. (*To the others*) We hardly ever see her—we're out so much, doing our charity work, you know, looking after sick animals etcetera etcetera. But give us her invitation. We'll make sure she gets it.
Donna She'll get it, all right.
Prince Charming Oh, well. That seems sensible. William, give the ladies Cinderella's invitation.
William Really? Shall I?

The object here is to get the audience shouting "No". Meanwhile the Uglies are trying to get hold of the invitation. Perhaps the Horse grabs it and passes it to Prince Charming

Prince Charming No. Perhaps not. Go and deliver it personally, William.
(*To the Uglies*) Well, now, if you'll excuse me . . .
Bella Don't dash, Princey, Billy, if I may be so bold. After all . . .

SONG 5: **Give us a Kiss!**

During the song the Ugly Sisters maul and manipulate Prince Charming and William, who react appalled, even disgusted. If desired, some lines can be sung solo

Bella ⎫
Donna ⎭
We couldn't have met by accident
Here in this lonely spot
It must be fate
So let's not wait
Let's strike while the iron is hot!

Give us a kiss!

Prince Charming ⎫
William ⎭
What?

Bella ⎫
Donna ⎭
A kiss.
Give us a try!
Give us a kiss!
Like this
Now don't be shy
Hold us close and you will see
We're as cuddly as girls can be
So go on!
Give us a kiss!

Prince Charming ⎫
William ⎭
We'd rather
Give it a miss.

Prince Charming and William try to escape, but are caught again

Bella ⎫
Donna ⎭
Give us a squeeze!

They grab the Prince and William

Prince Charming ⎫
William ⎭
AAAAH!

Bella ⎫
Donna ⎭
Oh please
Give us a thrill!
We're on our knees
One squeeze!
Oh say you will
Just relax, don't be straight-laced
Run your fingers around my waist
So go on!
Give us a squeeze!

Prince Charming ⎫
William ⎭   No thanks—

Bella ⎫   Oh!
Donna ⎭   Don't be a tease.

The Ugly Sisters chase the Prince and William off

The music continues as the Horse registers that everyone has gone. He takes the opportunity to do a soft shoe shuffle

As the dance finishes, the Ugly Sisters enter, carrying the Prince and William in their arms

Prince Charming ⎫   Ladies please
William ⎭   Put us down
                           To be frank we're not too keen
                           Ladies please
                           Put us down
                           For we don't know where you've been.

Bella ⎫   Give us a squeeze!
Donna ⎭

Prince Charming ⎫   No!
William ⎭

Bella ⎫   Oh please
Donna ⎭   Give us a break!
                           Nibble my ear

Prince Charming ⎫   No fear!
William ⎭

Bella ⎫   For pity's sake!
Donna ⎭   Hug us, woo us, do your stuff
Prince Charming ⎫   Ladies, listen, we've had enough!
William ⎭
Bella ⎫   Oh go on!
Donna ⎭   Give us a squeeze!
                           Give us a kiss!
                           Give us a try!—

Prince Charming ⎫   Ladies we give you—*GOOD-BYE!*
William ⎭

At the end of the song, there is either a BLACK-OUT, or the music continues while the Uglies exit, one dragging the sledge, one dragging the horse; and Prince Charming and William exit the other way—towards the Baron's Residence.

SCENE 4

The Baron's Kitchen

For variety, this scene could be in a formal, panelled room with a very large banqueting table, plus cupboard and door to outside; but there is no action here, or in the later Hall/Dining Room scene that could not logically take place in the Kitchen.

Cinderella is laying the table. She carries a large tray with a fruit bowl and cheese dish, which she unloads on to the table. She returns to the stove to stir a pot

Music (5a) as from behind the kitchen dresser a Mouse enters furtively. He checks all is safe, then runs sniffing till he catches the scent of the food on the table. He tries to climb on to the table but fails, then returns from whence he came, squeaks loudly, and beckons. A second Mouse—female—emerges. The first indicates the food, and they return to the table. One, helped by the other, climbs up, and takes some food, throwing some down for the other, too. A large lump of cheese. Suddenly they hear a noise—Cinderella turning—and in a flurry, leave the cheese and take shelter under the table, hidden by the table-cloth

Cinderella turns, unaware of what has happened. But suddenly she sees the cheese on the floor and registers surprise

Cinderella I knew it was *strong* cheese, but I didn't know it could jump! (*She picks it up*) How did you get down there, cheese?

The audience may shout out that two mice took it—if not, Cinderella asks them direct

A mouse? Two mice? Where are they now?

The audience tell her

Under the table? Are you sure? Thank you.

She lifts the tablecloth. The two Mice are huddled together, shaking violently. Cinderella calls to them, gently

Hey! Mice! Come out. I won't bite you. If you don't bite me.

Shy and embarrassed, the Mice, holding hands, edge out and stand sheepishly

Hello.

The Mice squeak shyly

Were you nibbling my cheese?

The Mice nod, and turn their heads away, ashamed

Why?

The Mice rub their stomachs to mime hunger. If required, Cinderella can ask the audience to interpret the mime

You were hungry?

The Mice nod

I'm not surprised. There's hardly enough food for us, let alone you two. Here you are.

She gives them the cheese. The Mice mime that they cannot *accept it*

Go on. It's the least I can do to help. And one day you can help me. All right?

The Mice nod, accept the cheese and give her a kiss, squeaking gratefully

Now, what are your names?

The Mice shrug their shoulders and mime they haven't got names

You *must* have names. Supposing I'm lonely one day and fancy a chat, I'll want to give you a call—but I'll need to know your names.

The Mice indicate the audience

What? Ask *them* to think of names for you? Good idea! (*To the audience*) Can anyone think of two nice names for two nice mice?

The audience shout out suggestions, which Cinderella puts to the Mice. At about the third attempt, they nod, accepting the names—which will probably be different at each performance. For the purpose of the script call them Johnny and Ginnie

Johnny and Ginnie? They like them!

SONG 6: **Squeak, Squeak, Squeak!**

Cinderella   We could keep each other company
                      Johnny and Ginnie, stay with me
                      I'll feed you each and ev'ry day
                      Johnny and Ginnie, say you'll stay.

(*To the audience*) I've just thought—you gave the mice their names, so why don't you join in and shout them out every time they come up in the song? Will you do that? Thank you. Let's have a practice. Shout out "Johnny and Ginnie". After three. One, two, three.

Audience Johnny and Ginnie!
Cinderella Lovely. Now I'll sing the song and when I wave, you shout the names.
    (*Singing*)   We could keep each other company
Cinderella }
Audience } Johnny and Ginnie

Cinderella   Stay with me.
                I'll feed you each and ev'ry day

| **Cinderella** } | Johnny and Ginnie |
| **Audience** | |

Cinderella   Say you'll stay.

Mice   Squeak, squeak, squeak!
Cinderella   Don't leave me little mice
                  Having friends like you
                  Would be extremely nice
Mice   Squeak, squeak, squeak!
Cinderella   Though you can't speak
                  I can understand you
                  When you
Mice   Squeak, squeak, squeak!

Cinderella   We could keep each other company

| **Cinderella** } | Johnny and Ginnie |
| **Audience** | |

Cinderella   Stay with me.
                  I'll feed you each and ev'ry day

| **Cinderella** } | Johnny and Ginnie |
| **Audience** | |

Cinderella   Say you'll stay.

Optional repeat of chorus

At the end of the song, there is a knock on the door. The Mice immediately panic, but Cinderella shows them under the table again. She goes to the door and opens it

William stands there

Cinderella Good morning.
William Good morning. Cinderella?
Cinderella (*surprised he knows her name*) Yes.
William An invitation. From the Palace. (*He hands it to her*)
Cinderella Oh. Thank you. It must be for my father and stepsisters.
William No. It's for you.
Cinderella Me? Oh, thank you.
William 'Bye. We'll look forward to seeing you.

William goes

Cinderella studies the invitation with excitement. The Mice peep from under the table cloth and squeak

Cinderella Safe to come out now. Look.

The Mice look at the invitation and squeak as if to say "What is it?"

It's an invitation to the Fancy Dress Ball at the Palace. I've always wanted to go there.

The Mice express their pleasure. Cinderella sighs

Never mind.

The Mice squeak questioningly

Well, I can't go. I've nothing to wear.

The Mice squeak and nod their heads, excitedly pointing out words on the invitation

What? Fancy dress?

They nod

No. I don't think they'd fancy *my* fancy dress.

The Mice squeak enquiringly

This. (*She indicates her tattered dress*) It's the only one I've got! (*Having an idea*) Unless I go as a poor kitchen maid!

The Mice nod and squeak enthusiastically

Anyway, Bella and Donna will never let me go, I bet.

The Mice look indignant, as if to say "Who?"

My stepsisters. They . . .

They are interrupted by voices outside

Bella (*off*) Cinderella!
Donna (*off*) Cinderella!
Cinderella Quick, mice, hide! Here they are!

The Mice scuttle under the table, shaking their fists at the door. Cinderella leaves her invitation on the table and answers the door

The Uglies enter, shattered by their exhausting trip to town. They carry large piles of Christmas-wrapped parcels

Bella Ooh, I'm shattered.
Donna My collies aren't wobbling any more. I think they've dropped off.
Bella Clear that rubbish off the table, Cinderella!
Cinderella I was laying it.
Bella (*imitating*) "I was laying it". You sound like a chicken. We need the space for our Christmas presents.
Cinderella Yes, Bella.

Cinderella clears some stuff off the table, not her invitation. The Uglies dump their parcels down, and each sorts through her own pile, reading labels

Bella ⎫ From you to me. (*Next parcel*) From ⎧ *Speaking*
Donna ⎭ Stepdaddy to me. (*Next one*) From me to me. ⎩ *together*
(*Picking up the next one*) From me to you.

Both turn to hand a parcel to each other, and crash the parcels into each other

Sorry. Happy Christmas, dear. Thank you. ⎰ *Speaking*
⎱ *together*

Donna I'm starving. Cinderella, where's our lunch?

Cinderella I was just . . .

Donna Don't answer back. I can't stand people who answer back. It's so rude.

Bella I should slap her hand, Donna. Teach her a lesson.

Donna Good idea, Bella. Come here.

Cinderella Please, Donna.

Donna Too late for please. Hold your hand out.

Cinderella does so; Donna goes to slap her. Suddenly, unseen by either of the Uglies, one of the Mice pops out from under the table and nips, gooses or hits Donna's rear. She jumps

Oo!

The Mouse retreats. Donna turns. Bella is standing there

Bella, really.

Bella What?

Donna How dare you?

Bella What?

Donna Pinch me.

Bella Don't be silly. Now, Cinderella, put these parcels under the Christmas tree, quickly.

Cinderella starts to pick up the parcels

And why isn't this table laid?

Cinderella I cleared it for your parcels.

Bella That's right, blame poor little me. Cheek. Come here. Hold your hand out.

Cinderella Please, Bella.

Bella Here.

Bella goes to slap Cinderella's hand. Out pops the other Mouse, and, unseen by the Uglies, pinches or bites Bella

Oo!

The Mouse disappears. Bella turns. Donna is standing there

Donna.

Donna What?

Bella How dare you!

Donna What?

Bella Pinch me.

Donna Don't be silly.

Cinderella leaves them to argue and clears the parcels away

Bella I'm not being silly.

Donna You are.

Bella I'm not.

They move downstage a bit, arguing

Cinderella exits when the parcels are cleared

Donna You are.
Bella I'm not. You pinched me.
Donna I didn't. You pinched *me*.
Bella Didn't.
Donna Did.
Bella Didn't.

During the above, the two Mice creep out of hiding, one to either side of the arguing Uglies, and pinch them again

Donna } Ow! { *Speaking*
Bella } { *together*

They turn outwards to see what pinched them, and the Mice scuttle away unseen. The Uglies walk in separate small circles, facing out, looking for their attackers. Eventually they bang into each other's backs

Ahh! { *Speaking*
{ *together*

The Uglies stop by the table, and suddenly spot Cinderella's invitation on it

(*Suspiciously*) Aaaaah! { *Speaking*
{ *together*

Bella I spy with my little eye—(*She picks it up*)
Donna —something beginning with I.
Bella An invitation—
Donna —to the Fancy Dress Ball . . .
Bella Is it yours, Donna?
Donna No. Is it yours, Bella?
Bella No. I think it must be—
Donna } Cinderella's! { *Speaking*
Bella } { *together*

They turn to the audience. As they do so, the Mice emerge from under the table and clamber up on it

Bella (*to the audience*) It *is* hers, isn't it?
Audience (*encouraged by the Mice*) No.
Donna Yes, it is.
Audience No, it isn't.
Bella Yes, it is. Do you think she'll want to go, Donna?
Donna No, Bella, she hates dancing and she loathes palaces and she can't stand parties.
Bella You're right, Donna. She won't want to go. Let's do her a favour and—tear up the invitation!
Donna (*laughing*) Yes, let's . . . (*To the audience*) shall we?
Audience No!
Donna Yes?
Audience No.
Bella } Yes! { *Speaking*
Donna } { *together*

Donna grabs it from Bella

Donna I'll do it.

Bella grabs it back

Bella No, Donna, I'll do it.

Donna grabs it and holds it overhead. The Mice start trying to grab it

Donna I want to tear it up.

Bella grabs it back, still holding it aloft

Bella I want to.
Donna Me.
Bella Me.
Donna Me.
Bella Me.

In the end, the invitation is taken by the Mice, and the Uglies continue swapping it from hand to hand without realizing it has gone, ad-libbing "me" or "mine" as necessary. The Mice jump off the table, leaving the invitation on the table, and hide underneath again

Donna (*realizing it has disappeared*) Where's it gone?
Bella You've got it.
Donna No, I haven't.
Bella Thief.
Donna Thief yourself.

They continue arguing

  Baron Hardy enters

Baron Girls, girls. (*He goes to intervene and narrowly escapes getting hit*) Break, break. (*He finds a bell on the dresser and rings it*)

The Uglies stop arguing

  End of Round One. (*He points*) Red Corner. Blue Corner. Now what are you fighting about?
Bella An invitation she stole.
Donna I didn't.
Baron Ssh. Ssh. Now. Invitation to what?
Donna To the Palace for a Christmas Fancy Dress Ball.
Bella We're all invited.
Baron How splendid . . . (*He spies the invitation on the table*) Ah! Is this what you were quarrelling about?
Bella } Yes { *Speaking*
Donna } { *together*

They grab, but the Baron keeps hold of it

Baron But this is addressed to Cinderella.

  Cinderella enters carrying a lunch tray, or pushing a trolley

  (*Seeing her, waving the invitation*) Isn't this exciting, dear?

Cinderella Yes, Father.
Baron I'm delighted for you.
Bella Such a shame.
Cinderella What?
Bella Such a shame you hate dancing.
Cinderella But I don't. I love dancing.
Donna Such a shame you loathe royal palaces.
Cinderella I don't. I've always wanted to see inside one.
Bella Such a shame you can't.
Cinderella Eh?
Donna Such a shame you can't go.
Baron But, girls. She's been invited. (*He holds up the invitation*)

Bella grabs it, and tears it into tiny pieces. A chilling hush

Bella (*smiling calmly*) Such a shame there's no admittance without a ticket.
Bella ⎫ Such a shame. ⎰ *Speaking*
Donna ⎭   ⎱ *together*

Cinderella nearly breaks down

Baron Oh, girls, what a cruel thing to do . . .
Bella Shut up, Stepdaddy.
Donna I'm starving. Serve, Cinderella.
Cinderella Yes, Donna.

The Uglies and the Baron sit at the table

Bella And after lunch you will kindly deliver to the Palace our replies to the
  Royal Family's kind invitation. Our *three* replies.
Cinderella Yes, Bella.
Baron Oh, girls, girls.
Donna Shut up, Stepdaddy.

*Cinderella serves the plates. Bella trips her deliberately, causing a whole plate
of food to tip up over Donna*

  Aaaaah! You horrid girl, you did that on purpose.
Cinderella I . . .
Bella Let's spank her, the vicious creature.

*The Uglies grab Cinderella and go to hit her. The two Mice pop out and the
Uglies see them for the first time. Donna drops Cinderella's hand in fright*

Bella ⎫ Aaaaah! Mice! Mice! Shoo! ⎰ *Speaking*
Donna ⎭ Help! etc.   ⎱ *together*

*Music as the Mice chase the Uglies, who hold up their skirts and run around
screaming, falling, bumping into each other, etc. Cinderella and the Baron
retreat. Eventually the Uglies leap on to the table in panic*

SONG 7: **Shoo!**

Bella ⎫   Shoo, shoo,
Donna ⎭   Be off with you
            You're dirty and dusty and mucky
            Shoo, shoo,
            Be off with you
            You're grubby and grimy and yucky
            The sight of the likes of you
            Offends the likes of us
            No wonder we're making a fuss
            Be off with you
            Shoo, shoo, shoo!

            You move in such frightening spurts
            You try to get under our skirts
            You're vicious and rude
            And you pinch all our food
            And then give us a nip where it hurts.

            Shoo, shoo,
            Be off with you
            You're dirty and dusty and mucky
            Shoo, shoo,
            Be off with you
            You're grubby and grimy and yucky
            The sight of the likes of you
            Offends the likes of us
            No wonder we're making a fuss
            Be off with you
            Shoo, shoo, shoo!

At the end of the song, the Mice chase the Uglies again till they collapse or faint: possibly chasing them around the auditorium.

SCENE 5

The Palace Courtyard, or a front-cloth depicting the Palace Cloister or Gardens

In the background a couple of Workmen are putting up Christmas decorations for the Ball, but they are not aware of what is happening in the scene, and do not distract attention from it

    Prince Charming enters, Hamlet-like, reading a book intently. He gets tangled up with a paperchain, but appears not to notice. He looks meaningfully at the Workmen, who leave. Having checked there is no-one about, he reads his book. With grim determination and very clumsy movement, he starts shuffling around in a very strange, stiff manner, concentrating furiously on the book

After a short while Cinderella enters. She carries the three invitation replies from the Hardy family. She stops when she sees the strange sight. He suddenly sees her watching him and is highly embarrassed

Prince Charming What are you doing?
Cinderella What are *you* doing?
Prince Charming I thought I was on my own.
Cinderella I'm sorry. (*She cannot help laughing*)
Prince Charming You don't sound it.
Cinderella I am, really. But, well, whatever you were doing was quite funny. Do you always do it when you're on your own?
Prince Charming It was dancing.
Cinderella Dancing? Oh. (*She nods helpfully*)
Prince Charming It's hopeless. I hate dancing, but I've got to go to the Fancy Dress Ball, so I thought I'd better learn. (*He holds up the book*) "Do-it-yourself Dancing Lessons." "Float across the floor with grace."
Cinderella Who's Grace?

Prince Charming looks at her and laughs

I love dancing.
Prince Charming You don't, do you? It's so—soppy. Foxtrots and fandangoes and slow, slow, quick, quick, slow ...
Cinderella It's not. I'll teach you the Funky Monkey if you like; that's not soppy. It's the latest craze.
Prince Charming Would you? Would you really?
Cinderella Why not? I'll be your "Grace".
Prince Charming Eh?
Cinderella "Float across the floor with Grace!" Come on ...

She takes his book and puts it down, putting her invitation replies with it

SONG 8: **The Funky Monkey**

During the first verse, Cinderella demonstrates the movements, encouraging the Prince to follow them

> You let your arms hang down
> You make a funny face
> You bend your knees
> And jump all over the place.
>
> Funky monkey
> Funky monkey
> Funky monkey
> Funky monkey

Others, including the Jester, Children, etc., enter, take in the scene and join in

> Pretend you're swinging through
> The branches of a tree
> And you can do
> The Funky Monkey with me.

By now the Prince has gained confidence

Cinderella ⎫	Funky monkey
Prince Charming ⎬	Funky monkey
Chorus ⎭	Funky monkey
	Funky monkey

And then you look around
To find your monkey match
And when you do
You have a jolly good scratch.

Funky monkey
Funky monkey
Funky monkey
Funky monkey
Funky monkey
Oh yeah!

The song ends. The audience will probably applaud. The music starts up again

All　　　　　　　　Funky monkey
　　　　　　　　　　Funky monkey ...

The King and Queen enter

King (*shouting*) Quiet!

All stop singing and dancing

Cease this appalling caterwauling. Charming, what on earth are you doing?
Prince Charming The Funky Monkey, Father.
King The Funky Monkey?
Cinderella Charming? Are you Prince Charming?
Queen Who's that dirty little creature? Put her down, dear, you don't know where she's been. Come to Mummy.
Prince Charming But Mother, you don't understand. She's teaching me to dance.
Queen I don't care what she's doing. She's grubby. You might catch something. Come here.
Prince Charming But Mother ...
King Quiet, Charming. Do as your mother says. (*To Cinderella*) And you. Clear off this minute.

SONG 8a: **Shoo!** (reprise)

King ⎫	Shoo, shoo,
Queen ⎬	Be off with you
	You're dirty and dusty and mucky
	Shoo, shoo,
	Be off with you
	You're grubby and grimy and yucky

The sight of the likes of you
Offends the likes of us
No wonder we're making a fuss
Be off with you
Shoo, shoo, shoo!

Your common and slovenly dress
Makes you an unspeakable mess
Our words we don't mince
For our son is a prince
And we hardly think you a princess.

King⎱
Queen ⎰ Shoo, shoo,
Chorus⎰ Be off with you
You're dirty and dusty and mucky
Shoo, shoo,
Be off with you
You're grubby and grimy and yucky
The sight of the likes of you
Offends the likes of us
No wonder we're making a fuss
Be off with you
Shoo, shoo, shoo!

Cinderella rushes off. The King and Queen exit, followed by everyone except Prince Charming

Prince Charming (*calling after Cinderella*) Come back, please! I want to invite you to the Ball! (*He gives up. To himself*) And I don't even know who she is.

The audience will probably tell him, in which case he repeats the name "Cinderella" and the Lights fade. If not, he goes to collect his book, and finds the envelope left by Cinderella. He opens it and reads

"Baron Hardy and his daughters Bella and Donna take pleasure in accepting ..." (*Realizing*) She must have been Cinderella!

Music. The Lights fade

SCENE 6

The Ugly Sisters' bedroom. Christmas Eve, the night of the Ball

There is a bed; also a dressing-table, stools, large hair drier and the usual appurtenances

Bella and Donna are discovered in dressing-gowns, combing their hair or spraying themselves with perfume. A Hairdresser attends to Donna; a Beautician attends to Bella

Hairdresser How's that, madam?

Donna Mmm, yes. It's sort of Italian, isn't it?
Bella Like a bowl of spaghetti, you mean.
Donna With a bit of French thrown in.
Bella Two French poodles fighting in the bowl of spaghetti.
Donna It's better than your moulting haystack anyway.
Bella How dare you!

They start to argue. Bella squirts Donna with a perfume spray

Beautician Ladies, please. We're trying to make you look more beautiful.
Bella You'll have a job making *us* look more beautiful.
Beautician Yes, but we enjoy a challenge.
Bella Cheek.
Donna (*to the Hairdresser*) I don't think this style suits my fine bone struc-
   ture. You'd better start again.
Hairdresser What style would madam like?
Donna Oh, I don't know. Something Christmassy.

*During the following conversation, the hairdresser works away and eventually
puts Donna under a large prop hair-drier*

Bella (*to the Beautician*) Well, don't just stand there. Do your job. Beautify
   me.
Beautician Very well, madam. First I suggest a face pack.
Bella What? Oh no, I don't think ...

*Too late: the Beautician smashes a sort of custard pie into her face and spreads
it round. She splutters*

Beautician And now, a body massage.
Bella Eh? No, I ...

*Too late: the Beautician lifts her up, throws her on the bed and vigorously
massages her. This is almost choreographed, with him man-handling her
deftly, ignoring her screams and gasps*

Beautician Exercises.

He hauls her up and forces her up and down

   Touch your toes. Touch your toes. Touch your toes.

*A loud noise—ripping material—stops the activity, as Bella bends over. Em-
barrassment*

Bella That's enough.
Beautician You have to suffer to be beautiful.
Bella Well, I've suffered quite enough, thank you. I asked for a beautician,
   not an all-in wrestler. (*She recovers*)

A bell rings

Hairdresser Aha. Madam is ready.

*He removes the drier. Donna's hair is bright green, shaped like a Christmas
tree or a Christmas pudding complete with holly sprig*

Charming!

Bella sees it and roars with laughter. Donna looks in the mirror

Donna Aaaaah!
Hairdresser Something Christmassy!

Baron Hardy enters amid the panic. He wears a cloak or coat.

Baron Nearly time to go, girls.
Bella We're nowhere near ready, Stepdaddy.
Baron Hurry, please. We mustn't be late.

The Baron exits

SONG 9: Tonight is the Night

During the introduction, the Ugly Sisters could remove their dressing gowns revealing their funny underwear. During the song, which should be done in front of tabs or a front cloth to facilitate the scene change, the Hairdresser and Beautician could help them into their ball dresses, pull their corsets tight, etc., or it may be considered better to save their Fancy Dress costumes for the Ball itself

Bella ⎫ We're all of a flurry
Donna ⎭ We're in such a hurry
           All fingers and thumbs and left feet
           We're in such a state
           'Cos we mustn't be late
           For this right royal Christmas treat.

Hairdresser and Beautician could join in singing to 'Ah'

           Tonight is the night
           We've been waiting for
           What a wonderful night it will be
           The music will play
           The dancers will sway
           And the Belle of the Ball will be me.

Bella and Donna glare at each other

           Tonight is the night
           We've been waiting for
           The most magical evening of all
           The night of a lifetime
           Awaits us
           The night of the Royal Ball.
All   The night of a lifetime
           Awaits us
           The night of the Royal Ball.

The music continues as they exit, and the scene changes

SCENE 7

The Baron's Kitchen. Night

MUSIC 9A

Cinderella is working. She takes a large round traditional Christmas pudding out of the oven. Suddenly she breaks down and starts to sob. Squeaks are heard, and the Mice enter, at first unseen by Cinderella. They look at her sympathetically, look at each other and decide to cheer her up. They approach and cuddle up to her

Cinderella Hello Johnny, hello Ginnie. (*She blinks back the tears*)

The Mice squeak

    You've come to cheer me up?

They nod

    Well, I certainly need cheering up. (*She breaks down again*)

The Mice decide to try and make her laugh. They do some acrobatic tricks or silly action. Cinderella laughs

    Thank you, little mice. I'm sorry I was crying.

The Mice squeak enquiringly

    I so wanted to go to the Ball—just one night of excitement and fun—with dancing and ...

Johnny immediately formally bows an invitation to dance. Ginnie squeaks a tune, and Johnny and Cinderella dance round

    Thank you, Johnny.

They bow to each other

    You dance very elegantly.

Johnny goes all coy

    Better than Prince Charming.

The Mice squeak enquiringly

    Didn't I tell you I met him? I taught him the Funky Monkey. Of course, I didn't know who he was till the King and Queen came along.

The Mice squeak, impressed

    Then they called me names and told me to clear off. But at least I met the Prince.

The Mice make lovey-dovey noises to tease her

    Don't be silly. But he *was* very nice—and normal—not like a Prince at all, really.

The Baron enters

Baron (*calling off*) Hurry up, girls, please.

Bella ⎫ (*off: calling*) Co—ming, Stepdaddy, ⎰ *Speaking*
Donna ⎭ stop fussing, etc.   ⎱ *together*

The Mice hide under the table

Baron (*embarrassed, to Cinderella*) Well, dear, we're off now ... (*Seeing the Christmas Pudding*) Mm, that looks good.
Cinderella Have a lovely time, Father.
Baron Oh, Cinderella, please ...
Cinderella I mean it. Have a lovely time. (*She kisses him*)
Baron I'd have a lovelier time if I could take you instead of those two monsters. It's wicked the way they treat you, wicked. (*Raising his voice*) They ought to be locked up.

Bella enters in her fancy dress finery, a cloak over the top

Bella (*having overheard*) What was that, Stepdaddy?

The Baron jumps, terrified

Baron Er—they ought to be locked up—the doors—I was telling Cinderella, Bella; the doors must be locked up after we go out.
Bella Mmm. And opened when we get back. So it's not worth you going to sleep, Cinderella. We'll give you a list of jobs to do instead. (*She goes to the door and calls raucously*) Donna! (*Turning back*) Don't dawdle, Stepdaddy, dear. Get the horse ready. We'll ride. You can walk.
Baron Yes, Bella. (*To Cinderella*) 'Bye, 'bye, dear. (*Under his breath*) I'll try to smuggle you home a lump of cake.

The Baron scuttles out

Bella meanwhile spots the Christmas pudding and goes to steal a chunk

Bella This looks tasty. (*She takes some and puts it in her mouth*)
Cinderella It's still—
Bella (*screaming*) OW! (*She indecorously gets rid of the scalding pudding*)
Cinderella —hot.

Bella You did that on purpose, you ...

Bella advances menacingly: but attention is drawn from her as the door opens

Donna enters in her fancy dress finery, a cloak over the top

Donna I'm ready! Fit for a prince!
Bella He'll have a fit when he sees you!
Donna Do you think he'll take one look and fall headlong?
Bella Yes. He'll faint with shock! I'm the one he fancies rotten.

Cinderella laughs

What are you giggling at, you insolent sauce-box?

Cinderella Nothing, Bella.

Bella (*imitating*) Nothing, Bella. Well, this'll wipe that silly grin off your ugly mug. Take down tonight's list of jobs.

Cinderella writes. Donna titivates, maybe looking in a mirror

    (*In one breath*) You can shovel the coal, dust the shelves, whitewash the walls, brush the house, polish the silver, weed the window-boxes, scrape the spuds, beat the blankets, shampoo my wig, feed the chickens and stuff the turkey. (*She collapses, out of breath*)

Cinderella Sorry, I didn't catch all that.

Bella (*exhausted*) Donna, tell her.

Donna (*who hasn't really been paying attention*) Oh. Yes, Bella. (*To Cinderella, also in one breath*) You can dust the coal, shovel the shelves, brush the spuds, scrape the window-boxes, stuff the silver, beat the walls, shampoo the chickens, feed her wig, weed the blankets, whitewash the horse—and polish the turkey.

Bella Well, near enough.

Cinderella Is that all?

Bella Don't be sarcastic with me, my girl. Hard work never did anyone any harm.

Cinderella It's certainly never done you two any harm.

Bella Exactly.

Cinderella Because you've never done any.

Bella (*nodding*) Because we've never done any ... (*Suddenly realizing*) What? Did you hear that, Donna?

Donna I did, Bella. What a cheek! Vicious vixen! Callous cat!

Bella Insolent insubordinate ingrate! Grab her, Donna; that deserves a good spanking.

Cinderella No, please ...

The Uglies grab her

Bella We'll teach you ...

Suddenly the Mice pop out and "attack" the Uglies, chasing them away from Cinderella

Donna }
Bella }   Aaaaah! Mice! Help! etc. { *Speaking together*

They rush to the back door to get out, and collide with each other in the panic. Finally the door is opened

    Dramatic chord, as we see an old lady in a black cloak standing in the doorway: it is the Fairy Godmother

Donna Who are you?

Bella Out of our way, old hag.

Fairy Godmother Ladies, please, I've come a long way. May I kindly have a glass of water?

Donna Push off.

Bella If you want some water, go jump in the lake!

Bella and Donna go, cackling with laughter

The Fairy Godmother turns to leave

Cinderella Hey! Don't go. I'll give you a glass of water.
Fairy Godmother You're very kind.
Cinderella (*helping her*) Come in and sit by the fire.

The Mice stay visible, but out of sight of the Fairy Godmother

Fairy Godmother Thank you, dearie.
Cinderella (*getting the water*) You must forgive my stepsisters.
Fairy Godmother Mmm?
Cinderella The two who were so rude to you. They're going to the Fancy Dress Ball at the Palace, so they're all excited and in a hurry.
Fairy Godmother So I noticed. (*She does not drink the water*)
Cinderella Would you like something to eat?
Fairy Godmother No, thank you, dearie. I'd like to know why *you're* not going to the Ball.
Cinderella Well, someone has to look after the house, and I have my friends to keep me company.
Fairy Godmother Friends? What friends?
Cinderella Johnny, Ginnie—come and say hello.

The Mice appear and formally bow and curtsy

You're not frightened of mice, are you?
Fairy Godmother Certainly not. Some of my best friends are mice. How do you do?

The Mice squeak

Now, tell me the truth. Why aren't you going to this Ball? You were invited, weren't you?

Cinderella is reluctant to speak, but the Mice mime the Uglies tearing up the invitation

(*Interpreting*) Her stepsisters tore up the invitation?

The Mice squeak

Well, where are the torn-up pieces? For heaven's sake, child, how can I help you if you won't help me to help you?

The Mice find the pieces in a wastepaper-basket

Good. Thank you, mice. Now, stand back. (*She concentrates and makes a magical pass at the wastepaper-basket*)

There is a flash, and a puff of smoke

Have a look now.

The Mice take out the invitation restored again. They excitedly take it to Cinderella

Cinderella But—how did you do that? It's magic!

Fairy Godmother My little secret. But you could have done it with sticky tape if you'd had any spirit. I'm disappointed in you, Cinderella.

Cinderella How do you know my name?

Fairy Godmother Oh, she's slow. (*To the Mice*) Isn't she slow? Of course I know your name. I helped give it to you at your christening.

Cinderella My godmother?

Fairy Godmother Got it at last. Or nearly.

Cinderella My—*fairy* godmother?

Fairy Godmother At your service, dearie.

Cinderella But ...

Fairy Godmother But you don't believe in fairies? Mmm?

Cinderella nods, embarrassed

That's one reason why I'm here. I heard through the grapevine you were a non-believer, and thought I'd better fly over and knock some sense into you.

Cinderella But—you don't look like a fairy.

Fairy Godmother Oh, I see. Demonstration time is it? Some people are never satisfied. Right. Here goes. Stand back. (*She positions herself, makes a magical pass*).

Black-out. Flash. When the Lights come up the Fairy Godmother is revealed in all her fairy splendour, with magic wand. The Mice clap and squeak

Pretty impressive, eh?

Cinderella I can't believe it ...

Fairy Godmother There you go again!

Cinderella I'm sorry, but ...

Fairy Godmother I know, dearie. It's my fault. I should have come to see you more often. But I know all about your rotten stepsisters and the sorry old life you've been leading, so I'm giving you a special Christmas present.

Cinderella Thank you. (*She kisses the Fairy Godmother*)

Fairy Godmother No time for that. Now then, you'd better get going. If you waste any more time you'll arrive in the middle of the last waltz.

Cinderella You mean I can go to the Ball?

Fairy Godmother Why not? You've got an invitation.

Cinderella How will I get there?

Fairy Godmother Mm. Yes. Better do the job properly. You'll need a coach and horses and footmen and ... right. Something round. A pumpkin?

Or—(*seeing the Christmas pudding*)—that Christmas pudding will do splendidly. Take it outside, dearie, and put it in the yard. And look for some lizards, please.

Cinderella Lizards?

Fairy Godmother Yes. And a frog. I can magic very good footmen from lizards, and a coachman from a frog.

Cinderella exits by the back door

Now, horses. How can I magic horses?

The Mice squeak and run forward

What? You'd like to help Cinderella?

They nod

Of course you would. Off you go then.

The Mice rush out, meeting Cinderella at the door

Cinderella I've found some lizards. And a frog. (*She hands them to the Fairy Godmother*)

(*Optional: A small child could play the Frog*)

Fairy Godmother Ugh. Don't give them to me. They're all slimy.
Cinderella Sorry.
Fairy Godmother Put them down with the pudding and the mice—and then you'd better come back in, dearie. Pretty powerful stuff, this!

Cinderella goes

The Fairy Godmother looks about, then turns off the main light

Bit of atmosphere.

Cinderella returns. In fact, it is a "double" to allow Cinderella to change into her ballgown. The low lighting helps to disguise the deception

Sit down here, dearie.

"Cinderella" sits, with her back to audience

SONG 9B: **At the End of the Tunnel** (reprise)

Fairy Godmother Never lose sight
Of the speck of light
At the end of the tunnel
It's burning bright
Never lose faith
Never give up hope
At the end of the tunnel
You'll be all right.

Believe in your dreams
Whatever you do
Believe in your dreams
And they'll all come true ...

As the song ends, the Fairy Godmother takes a pose, and, if possible, a magical ripple effect spreads across the set. Music for tension

Christmas pud, frog, lizards and mice
Get ready to change, to change in a trice;
My magic power commands you all—
Take Cinderella to the Fancy Dress Ball! (*She waves her wand*)

Flash. Black-out

Optional: Music. A screen flies in and we see a filmed cartoon sequence of the transformation of the pudding, frog, lizards and mice into coach, coachmen, footmen and horses. The Fairy Godmother and "Cinderella" are in view watching, too.

Black-out. The screen flies out revealing the real coach, coachman, horses and footmen

---

If possible the set divides, or part of it slides or flies out, to reveal Cinderella's coach, coachman, horses and footmen. Music as a Footman comes forward and beckons "Cinderella" towards the coach. She stands and maybe shows reluctance by holding out her ragged skirt

Hang on! You can't go to the Palace in a coach like that looking like something the cat brought in. Close your eyes and hold tight, Cinderella. (*She takes a pose*) Cinderella's looking a right old mess; by magic let's make her a brand new dress. (*She waves her wand*).

Flash. Black-out

The real Cinderella, in stunning ballgown, changes places with the double

The Lights come up on the delighted Cinderella

Cinderella It's perfect! Thank you, Fairy Godmother. I believe now, I really do.
Fairy Godmother About time, dearie.

Cinderella starts towards the coach

Optional
Hang on a second time! Shoes. If you're going dancing you'll need a special pair of dancing shoes. Glass slippers made by the gnomes/elves of Fairy-land. (*She waves her wand*)

Children dressed as Gnomes or Elves enter and to music, create a pair of glass slippers, and present them to Cinderella, who slips them on

---

Cinderella gets in the coach, helped by a footman. Music continues over the next speech

Have a wonderful time, Cinderella. You deserve it. But just you remember one thing. My magic runs out at midnight. At twelve o'clock your coach will turn back to a pudding, your coachman to a frog, your footmen to lizards and your horses to mice. So whatever you do, be back here before the clock strikes twelve, or you'll be in a real pickle. Promise?
Cinderella I will, Fairy Godmother. And thank you. Thank you for the best Christmas present I could ever be given.

Fairy Godmother Pleasure, dearie. All part of the service. Now, be off with you!

SONG 9C: **Tonight is the Night** (reprise)

All ⎫	Tonight is the night
(including ⎪	You've been waiting for
offstage ⎬	The most magical evening of all
singers) ⎭	The night of a lifetime
	Awaits you
	The night of the Royal Ball.

The (optional) Gnomes and the Fairy Godmother wave good-bye. The coach starts to move as—

the CURTAIN falls

ACT II

The Ballroom at the Palace

It is a glittery occasion, with Christmas decorations, a chandelier if possible, and a staircase with an entrance on both sides, down which the Guests arrive. There is also a Christmas tree with presents. A large clock points to 11.30

MUSIC 10. *As the* CURTAIN *rises dancing is in progress. The couples include the King and Queen and William. Older children can play Ball Guests, younger ones Pages. All the Guests, and the King and Queen, are in fancy dress. The King is dressed as a lion. The Jester stands at the top of the stairs like a major-domo*

After a few bars, the Jester strikes a gong, or a staff on the floor, to gain attention

Jester My lords, ladies and gents. Superior snackettes and cordials are served in the saloon, In other words, this way for posh nosh and squash.

Laughter

A few guests exit, returning during the scene

Queen Oh, this *is* fun. I'm having a ball. (*She realises she has made a pun, and laughs*) Ha ha. Having a ball!

King (*not amused*) Yes, dear. I had noticed. I must say I don't think the fancy dress thing was a very good idea. (*He looks at himself gloomily*)

Queen Nonsense, Septimus, it's a roaring success. (*She looks at the King—a lion—and realizes the pun*) Ha ha. Roaring success! (*She roars lion-like*) King of the jungle!

King (*not amused*) Ha ha. I feel an absolute twit, I'm boiling hot and people keep treading on my tail.

Queen Where's Charming?

King If he's got any sense, he's gone out for the evening.

Queen (*calling*) William, fetch the Prince.

William Yes, Your Majesty.

William goes to the Christmas tree, behind which Prince Charming is sitting reading a book. He is not in fancy dress. Reluctantly he emerges

Queen Charming, you're a naughty boy. Why aren't you mingling?

Prince Charming Mingling, Mother?

King With your guests, boy. Your mother's arranged this do for *you*. To meet people. So mingle this minute.

Prince Charming But I ...

He is interrupted by the Jester banging for attention

Jester The Baron Hardy.

Fanfare

> *The Baron enters and walks down the steps*

King Ah. The frightened rabbit.
Baron (*nervously*) I beg your pardon, Your Majesty?
King (*shaking hands*) Er—I said—delightful habit—you are wearing. Good to see you, Hardy.
Baron (*shaking hands with the Queen*) Honoured, Your Majesties.
Jester The Lady Bella. And the Lady Donna.

> *The Uglies, in fancy dress, enter individually. Bella manages the stairs, but Donna trips down, knocking over Bella at the bottom*

Queen Welcome.

The Uglies get up and shake hands, and curtsy grotesquely

Bella Your majestics.
Donna Your soyal lubjects.

The Uglies get stuck on the floor, and the Baron has to help them rise

King Have you met our son, Charming?
Bella Indeed we have! Haven't we, Princy?
Donna We're thick as thieves.
Prince Charming Thick as two planks, if you ask me.

The Uglies roar with laughter

Bella Oh, he's a scream, he really is.
Donna He thinks he's such a wit!
Bella Pity he's only half right!

They shriek with laughter and playfully nudge the Prince

Prince Charming Have you brought your sister?
Bella
Donna } (*indicating each other*) Yes, we're both here! { *Speaking together*
Prince Charming No, Cinderella.
Baron Alas, Your Highness ...
Bella (*interrupting*) Alas, no. She refused to come. We tried, how we tried, didn't we, Donna?
Donna Tried?
Bella To persuade her to come.
Donna Oh yes. We tried. How we tried.
Bella But she just couldn't be bothered. Lazy little devil.
Baron But, girls ...
Bella
Donna } Shut up, Stepdaddy. { *Speaking together*

Jester (*banging for attention*) Your Majesties, my lords and ladies and gents, kindly take your partners for a tango.

MUSIC 11 The Ugly Tango

Prince Charming (*making to go*) Excuse me, ladies.
Bella }
Donna } We'd love to! { *Speaking together*
Prince Charming What?
Bella }
Donna } Tango. { *Speaking together*
Prince Charming But ...

He is too late, and is swept off his feet by the Uglies, who dance an energetic tango, pulling Prince Charming to and from each other. The Guests either watch, amused, or dance the tango too. After a while, the Prince, who has reluctantly been forced to be thrown around, is exhausted. The tango finishes in confusion. The Jester bangs for attention, then clucks in confusion

Jester Er—er—Your Majesties—er—er ...
King What's the matter, Jester? Are you laying an egg?
Jester No, Your Majesty, but ...
Queen Who has arrived?
Jester Er—er—a lady, Your Majesty, but I don't know who she is ...

Music

   Cinderella enters—a vision of loveliness

Everyone's attention turns towards the staircase; they whisper excitedly about the new arrival, wondering who she is: gasps of admiration

Kind (*admiringly*) Who is she?
Queen I've no idea. Did you invite her, Charming?
Prince Charming No, mother.
Baron She's quite lovely, isn't she girls?
Bella Mm. *Quite* lovely.
Donna If you like that sort of thing.

Cinderella reaches the bottom of the staircase and is greeted by the King and Queen

King You are most welcome.
Queen Indeed you are. Charming, greet your guest.
Prince Charming But she's *not* my ... (*He is shy, and mumbles*) How do you do?
Cinderella Your Highness.

The Jester bangs for attention

Jester Your Majesties, my lords, ladies and gents, kindly take your partners for a waltz!
Queen (*whispering to Prince Charming*) Go on, dear, ask her to dance. (*She prods him*)

Prince Charming Er—would you—er ...
Cinderella I'd be honoured, sir.

MUSIC 12 The Christmas Waltz

Prince Charming and Cinderella take the floor. Others join in

Bella What a cheek! Who does she think she is? He was dancing with us.
Donna Gatecrashes the party and grabs the main attraction. What a nerve!

Bella and Donna look around, find themselves on their own, shrug their shoulders and start to dance with each other. Prince Charming dances clumsily. He and Cinderella arrive C. He treads on her foot. She reacts

Prince Charming Oh, I'm sorry. I'm not very light on my toes.
Cinderella You're not very light on *my* toes, Your Highness.

She laughs. They start waltzing again

Prince Charming You know, I'm sure we've met before.
Cinderella Maybe we have.
Prince Charming I know. You're a princess. I met you at one of those royal dos when we were children! A coronation or something! You're a princess.
Cinderella If you say so, Your Highness.

He steps on her foot again

Ouch! I think I'm cramping your style.
Prince Charming No. I've no style for you to cramp. I'm hopeless at dancing. Except one dance I've just learned.
Cinderella What's that?
Prince Charming The Funky Monkey. It's all the rage, apparently. You don't know it, do you?
Cinderella (*concealing the irony of the question*) Well ...
Prince Charming It's quite tricky.
Cinderella I'm willing to try. If you show me how.
Prince Charming All right! (*He shouts*) Stop the music.

All stop dancing. Prince Charming rushes up to the Jester and whispers in his ear. He returns to Cinderella as the Jester makes his announcement

Jester Your Majesties, my lords, ladies and gents. By Royal Command, take your partners for the Funky Monkey.

Music starts, as everybody positions themselves. The King and Queen and the Uglies look uncertain about dancing this energetic dance, but decide to have a go

SONG 12A: The Funky Monkey (reprise)

All, including William, sing and dance. Prince Charming really comes into his own with Cinderella: they thoroughly enjoy themselves

All   You let your arms hang down
You make a funny face
You bend your knees
And jump all over the place

Funky Monkey
Funky Monkey
Funky Monkey
Funky Monkey

Pretend you're swinging through
The branches of a tree
And you can do
The Funky Monkey with me

Funky Monkey
Funky Monkey
Funkey Monkey
Funky Monkey

And then you look around
To find your monkey match
And when you do
You have a jolly good scratch

Funky Monkey
Funky Monkey
Funky Monkey
Funky Monkey
Funky Monkey
Oh yeah!

*By the end of the song and dance, the Uglies are quite exhausted and collapse.
Other Guests relax. The Baron chats to the King and Queen. Cinderella goes
to the Uglies, and graciously helps them up*

Bella Hands off, whoever you are.
Cinderella I'm sorry. I thought the Funky Monkey may have been too
energetic for you.
Donna (*breathless and wheezing*) Nonsense. I could have Funky Monkied
all night and still have begged for—mercy! (*She collapses again*)
Bella (*to Cinderella*) Clear off, clever-clogs. I'll have you know *we* were
dancing with Prince Charming when you barged your way in. You know
what you are, don't you. You're a—(*thinking of the worst possible insult-
ing phrase*)—you're a ...

Meanwhile, Prince Charming has summoned William

Prince Charming William. Kindly fetch some refreshment for the Princess.
Bella You're a ...
William Certainly, Your Highness.

William bows and exits

Bella (*continuing*) You're a ... (*realizing*) PRINCESS?

Both Uglies immediately change tack and fall fawning at Cinderella's feet

Bella ⎱ Oh, your gracefulness; your loveliness; what an ⎰ *Speaking*
Donna ⎰ honour, etc.   ⎱ *together*
Cinderella Please get up.
Bella ⎱ Oh, thank you; she's so genteel, isn't she? ⎰ *Speaking*
Donna ⎰ What a smasher, etc.   ⎱ *together*
Cinderella Shall we sit down?
Bella Why not?
Donna Charmed, I'm sure.

With mock elegance, the Uglies lead Cinderella to a table and two chairs. Both take a chair and offer it to Cinderella

Bella Allow me.
Donna Allow me.
Bella Sit on mine.
Donna Sit on mine.
Bella Mine.
Donna Mine.
Bella I asked first.
Donna My chair's nicer than yours.
Bella It's not. It wobbles.
Donna It doesn't wobble.
Bella Does.
Donna Doesn't.
Bella Shut up.
Donna Shut up yourself.
Cinderella Ladies, please!

The Uglies return to mock elegance

Bella So sorry.
Donna Pardon.

Both rush in with their chairs. Cinderella sits on Bella's. Bella makes a rude face at Donna as if to say "I won". Bella goes to sit on Donna's chair. At the last moment Donna pulls it away. Bella sits on the floor. Donna laughs, and prepares to sit on her chair. Bella kicks it out of the way. Donna sits on the floor alongside Bella

   William enters with a plate or tray of goodies

William Your refreshment, Your High...
Bella Oh thank you, Billy boy.
Donna You're a brick.

They grab the food and start eating

William It wasn't for you, it was for the Princess.
Bella Oh. Beg pardon.
Donna Silly us.

They put back all the food, mangled and squeezed, and hand it to Cinderella

Bella So sorry.
Donna Pardon.
Cinderella I don't think I'll bother.
Bella Oh well...
Donna In that case...

The Uglies start stuffing their faces

Cinderella Aren't you Baron Hardy's stepdaughters?

The Uglies nod and grunt a "yes"—their mouths are full

Bella?
Bella (*mouth full, spraying pastry everywhere*) Bella. That's me.
Cinderella And Donna?
Donna (*mouth full*) Donna. That's me.
Cinderella I've heard so much about you.

Bella } (*making appreciative sounds, mouths still (full*) { *Speaking*
Donna } Mmmm? Ohhh?   { *together*
Cinderella And your other sister.

Both Uglies explode. Pastry flies everywhere

Bella (*eventually*) What?
Donna Who?
Cinderella Your sister. Well, stepsister. Cinderella.
Bella Who?
Donna Cinderella.
Bella (*sotto voce*) Shut up, I heard. (*Aloud, to Cinderella*) Thin umbrella?
Cinderella No. Cinderella.
Bella Oh. Her. Yes. Well. She's got measles.
Cinderella Really?
Bella Yes. Spotty as a dalmation, she is. (*To Donna*) Isn't she?
Donna Eh? Oh yes, spotty as an alsatian.
Bella She looked in the mirror and she was so ugly she decided she couldn't
   come or she'd frighten all the guests away. Mind you, she was ugly *before*
   she had measles. She *is* ugly. Isn't she, Donna?
Donna Eh?
Bella Ugly.
Donna Revolting.
Bella } Disgusting. Ugh! (*To the audience*) Isn't she? { *Speaking*
Donna }   { *together*
Audience No.
Bella } There you are! { *Speaking*
Donna }   { *together*
Jester (*banging for attention*) Your Majesties, my lords, ladies and gents,
   kindly take your partners for the Christmas Waltz.

Music starts. The clock is approaching midnight

Prince Charming appears and walks towards the Uglies and Cinderella

The Uglies get up, thinking he is going to dance with them, but he makes straight for Cinderella. The Uglies, furious, look round. One grabs the Baron, the other grabs William

SONG 12B: **The Christmas Waltz**

All sing and dance. During the song the Lights narrow on to a happy Prince Charming and Cinderella: another spot picks out the clock

All	While the seconds are ticking away To Christmas Day Let's celebrate This special date In an old-fashioned way.

A time to forget, a time to forgive
A time for living and letting live

For the season of good will and cheer
Is nearly here
And if only the spirit of Christmastime
Could last throughout the year

Prince Charming ⎫ Yes if only the spirit of Christmastime
Cinderella ⎭ Could last throughout the year.

At the end of the song a loud chime is heard. It is midnight

Jester (*stopping the music by banging for attention*) Your Majesties, my lords, ladies and gents. It's Christmas Day!

Second chime

All cheer and break from dancing to say "Happy Christmas" to each other

Third chime

Cinderella is included in the celebration

Fourth chime

More "Happy Christmas" warmth

Fifth chime

Suddenly, Cinderella realizes midnight is approaching. She looks at the clock

Sixth chime

Tension music. Cinderella starts to try to exit, but is stopped by the King and Queen wishing her "Happy Christmas"

Seventh chime

Jester Your Majesties, my lords, ladies and gents. Time to sing a seasonal greeting.

Eighth chime

Music starts, as all hold hands "Auld Lang Syne" style. Cinderella looks for escape, but cannot find a way through

Ninth chime

As the chime strikes, all start singing

All   We wish you a Merry Christmas

Tenth chime

We wish you a Merry Christmas

Eleventh chime

We wish you a Merry Christmas and a Happy New Year.

As all sing, Cinderella trips, dropping a glass slipper on the staircase, then staggers off—in the wrong direction. The Jester tries to stop her, but she disappears

Twelfth chime

All applaud and cheer

In a spot, at the top of the staircase, Cinderella's "double", in the "rags" costume, dashes across to the correct exit and disappears

The Jester does not see this

Prince Charming (*shouting above the noise*) Where's the princess?

All look round for her

Jester Your Highness, she ran out. I tried to stop her, but she was in a terrible state ...

Prince Charming William, try and find her.

William dashes up the stairs and is shown off, in the wrong direction, by the Jester

(*calling*) And William, you can tell everyone I will offer a reward to anyone who can bring her back to me.

The King and Queen look pleased at their son's new attitude

Bella ⎫ Ooh? How much? Reward! Quick, after her. Shift ⎰ *Speaking*
Donna ⎭ your chassie, dear, etc.   ⎱ *together*

Bella and Donna run out, up the stairs, in pursuit, following William off the wrong way

Baron (*highly embarrassed*) Girls, please. Where are your manners? Come back. (*To the King and Queen*) Your Majesties, please forgive them. I'd lock them up, only they'd chew through the bars. (*Running off in pursuit*) Girls, please.

The Baron exits, bumping into the returning William

William (*breathlessly*) No sign, Your Highness.
Prince Charming Well, don't give up, William. Keep searching.

William runs off in the correct direction, pursued across the landing by the Uglies, in turn chased by the Baron. All exit

King Splendid, splendid. The lad's showing a bit of gumption at last. (*To Prince Charming*) That's the spirit, my boy.
Queen Good boy, Charming, good boy.
Prince Charming Please. Don't interrupt. This is important.
King Bravo, bravo. (*To the Queen*) My little plan worked, Ermintrude.
Queen What?
King My little plan to hold a Fancy Dress Ball where Charming could meet people ...
Queen I beg your pardon—*my* little plan ...

They continue arguing

William enters

William (*even more breathlessly*) Still no sign, Your Highness.
Prince Charming Didn't you see *anyone*?
William Just a poor serving-girl hanging around outside the Palace. She ran off when she saw me.
Prince Charming Go back again. She *must* be somewhere.

William staggers off

The Jester spots the glass slipper, picks it up and hands it to Prince Charming

Jester Your Highness.
Prince Charming A glass slipper.

Prince Charming looks at the slipper thoughtfully, as the music intensifies

Black-out

SCENE 2

The Chase

A cloth flies in, or blacks as the chase is taking place at night

The sequence should be an amusing chase across the stage to show how eventually Cinderella and the Mice "escape" their pursuers. It could be done as a "silent film", with strobe lighting effect, or as a straight-forward chase with exciting music. Below is a suggested framework.

1. The Mice enter, R, look tentatively about, then beckon on Cinderella from R. She is in her "rags" costume. They exit L
2. Bella enters, R in pursuit. She stops C, to check her bearings. Donna enters R, head down on the run; she hurtles into Bella, who reacts angrily, then indicates off L. Both exit L
3. The Baron enters R, chasing the Uglies: he staggers off L
4. William enters R. He crosses and exits L

5. The Mice and Cinderella enter L and exit R, pursued in near proximity by the Uglies, Baron and William. All exit R

6. Cinderella and the Mice enter R. They reach three-quarters of the way across the stage, when the Uglies enter R. Cinderella stops while the Mice run back and frighten the Uglies in a funny way. The Mice then turn back and escort Cinderella off L. Meanwhile the Uglies have turned round in panic, having been frightened. They run back R, and run into the Baron who enters R. The Uglies turn him round in their panic and all exit R

7. William enters R downstage of the exiting trio; he scratches his head and pauses to consider his next move. Suddenly the Uglies and the Baron enter at speed R. William reacts, and is forced to run off L, pursued by the Uglies and the Baron

8. Cinderella and the Mice enter L, downstage of the exiting group in 7. They look behind them and see the others approaching. The Mice, having an idea, pose statue-like centre-stage, and Cinderella hides behind them. William enters L and exits R, not noticing the "statue". The Uglies enter L. The Mice "come to life" and frighten the Uglies again in another funny way. The Uglies react in terror, turn and go to exit L. Meanwhile the Mice return to their "statue" position to hide Cinderella. As the Uglies approach the wings, the Baron enters L; he bumps into the fleeing Uglies. They wave their arms about, arguing over which way to go, and eventually all start heading R. As they cross the half-way mark, William enters R; he bumps into the other three and all fall over and roll helplessly on the floor. This gives Cinderella and the Mice their chance to escape safely L, leaving a tossing and tangled heap of four bodies trying to get up and falling over again

Black-out

SCENE 3

The Baron's Kitchen

The Fairy Godmother is asleep in a chair, not very visible

> *The Mice and Cinderella enter. She is breathless and exhausted from her run, but radiant. She still wears one glass slipper. The Mice lead her to a chair, sit her down and wave handkerchiefs or teacloths in her face, like a boxer's seconds, to revive her*

Cinderella Oh, thank you, Johnny and Ginnie. I thought we'd never get back safely.

A voice startles them

Fairy Godmother (*from the chair*) So did I. It's nearly morning.
Cinderella Oh, it's you, Fairy Godmother. Sorry. I didn't expect you to be here still.
Fairy Godmother Of course I'm still here. I want to know how it all went.
Cinderella It was wonderful. (*To the Mice*) Wasn't it?

The Mice shrug their shoulders and almost look resentful, squeaking crossly

Oh, sorry, I forgot. (*To the Fairy Godmother*) They were furious because they missed it all.

Fairy Godmother Why?

Cinderella They were horses, so they were stuck in the stables all night.

Fairy Godmother Oh, dear. Never thought of that. Sorry, mice.

The Mice bow politely

(*To Cinderella*) But *you* had a good time, eh?

Cinderella (*sincerely*) Yes, thank you. It was the happiest night I can ever remember. (*She kisses the Fairy Godmother*).

Fairy Godmother Get away with you, dearie.

Cinderella Thank you. And Merry Christmas! I wish I could give you as nice a present as you gave me.

Fairy Godmother Rubbish. You've made an old fairy *very* merry! Now, tell me all about it. Why are you so late?

Cinderella Well, I got so carried away, before I knew it the clock started striking twelve; so I ...

She is interrupted by the sound of the Uglies and Baron returning offstage—groans of discomfort, etc. All freeze; then begins a frenzy of activity and sign language. The two Mice wave good-bye and retreat under the table or behind the sideboard dresser. Cinderella shows the Fairy Godmother to the door leading to the rest of the house. Then she thinks better of it, and puts her behind the back door, indicating she should slip out after the others have come in. Swiftly Cinderella locks and bolts the door. Immediate knocking and shouting from outside—"Cinderella, open up"—etc. Cinderella suddenly remembers her glass slipper, takes it off, and hides it—in the fireplace, where the Baron's moneybox was found in Act 1. Then she unlocks the door and opens it, thus virtually hiding the Fairy Godmother from view

The bedraggled Uglies enter, supported by the ailing Baron

Baron Thank you, dear. Sorry we're late.

Bella Ohhhhhhhhhhhhhh!

Donna Water! Water!

During the above the Fairy Godmother creeps round to the open door, and turns back into the room, unseen by the others

Fairy Godmother Go *jump* in the *lake*!

The Fairy Godmother exits quickly and shuts the door

Donna Eh?

Bella What?

They turn back to see Cinderella bolting the door. They assume it was she talking

Cinderella Er—lump of—cake. Did you get me a lump of cake?

Bella Certainly not, you greedy hog.

The Uglies flop against the table or sit down. The Baron watches helplessly as usual

Cinderella Did you have a good evening? Did you dance with Prince Charming?

Donna Dance with him? We wiped the floor with him! Didn't we, Bella?

Bella Yes. (*Giving orders*) Water, Stepdaddy.

The Baron jumps to attend to her

Optional

He had eyes only for us. He said if we hadn't been there, it wouldn't have been the same.

Cinderella Mmm. I know what he means.

Bella What?

Cinderella (*changing the subject*) Anyone else exciting there?

Donna No, only us. Oh, and that snooty stuck-up Princess.

Cinderella Princess?

Bella Yes. Very upper crust, she was. Spent most of her time chatting us up, trying to impress us.

Cinderella What did she look like?

Donna All right.

Bella Not bad.

Baron Oh, girls, be fair. She was stunning. Pretty as a picture.

Bella A horror picture!

Donna Ha, ha, ha.

Baron She was lovely. Actually she rather reminded me of you.

Bella ⎫
Donna ⎬ Oh, thank you, Stepdaddy. { *Speaking together*

Baron Not you two. Cinderella.

Bella Her?

Donna Her?

Bella ⎫ Hah! { *Speaking
Donna ⎬   together*

Bella There's no comparison.

Donna No. The Princess wasn't up to much, but compared with Cinderella she was Miss Universe. Cinderella's so ugly, they wouldn't have let her in the door.

Bella Even if she'd had an invitation.

And why, Cinderella, haven't you done those jobs, eh?

Donna Yes, why haven't you polished the turkey?

Cinderella Er—I've been rather busy.

Bella Busy? That's the one thing you haven't been, busy. (*Looking around*) And where's that Christmas pudding? I just fancy some.

Cinderella It—er—I've eaten it.

Bella You've *eaten* it?

Donna All of it?

Cinderella No, I—er—shared it. With a friend.

Donna She shared it with a friend.

Bella How dare you share it with a friend!
Donna How dare you have a friend to share it with!
Bella Get her!
Donna Come here!

They chase Cinderella round, trying to grab her. Eventually the Mice run out and chase off the Uglies, who have to leap over the table, etc. in panic

The Uglies exit through the door to the rest of the house

The Mice go to Cinderella to guard her

Baron Happy Christmas, dear.
Cinderella I'm having one, Father. Tonight is a night I'll never forget.
Baron I just wish you could have come to the Ball, that's all.
Cinderella That's what I did. Wished.

This is too enigmatic for the Baron to understand

Baron Good night, dear.
Cinderella 'Night, Father.

They embrace

The Baron exits

MUSIC 12A. *The Mice yawn and stretch. Cinderella smiles and leads them to the fireside. All three start to huddle together, then Cinderella goes to the fireplace and takes out the glass slipper. She lowers the lights, and sits down, with the Mice at her feet*

SONG 13: **One Glass Slipper**

Cinderella   One glass slipper
                   Is all I have
                   To remind me of a magic time
                   One glass slipper
                   A souvenir
                   Of a dream that had to end on midnight's chime.

The music continues, and Cinderella moves downstage as the scene changes; remaining onstage

SCENE 4

The Palace Courtyard, or a front-cloth depicting the Palace Cloister or Gardens. The next day, Christmas morning

The decorations for the Ball are still in position

Prince Charming is discovered sitting on a convenient bench, singing a continuation of Cinderella's song. He carries the other glass slipper. Cinderella, in her own light, is obviously not really part of the scene, and neither she nor Prince Charming acknowledge the other's presence

SONG 13 (*continuation*) **One Glass Slipper**

Prince Charming   One glass slipper
                            Is all I have
                            To remind me of a magic night
                            One glass slipper
                            The only trace
                            Of a vision that has vanished out of sight.

Prince Charming ⎱   One glass slipper
Cinderella   ⎰   Is all I have
                            To remind me of a dream come true
                            One glass slipper
                            Is all I have
                            To remind me of you.

Cinderella exits

Prince Charming remains sitting and hoping

The King, Queen and Jester enter from the opposite side

The Jester points out where Prince Charming sits

Jester (*in a loud whisper*) He's been there ever since last night, Your Majesties.
Queen Oh, Charming. Baby. He'll get pneumonia.
King He'll get a black eye if he doesn't snap out of it. Fat lot of good your Fancy Dress Ball idea was. It's made him even worse.
Queen He's always been moody. Even when he was little. (*Enjoying the reminiscence*) I used to cheer him up by bouncing him up and down on my knee and giving him a jellybaby.
King Mm. Well, I can't quite see that cheering him up today.
Queen No. Anyway, I haven't any jellybabies.
King Go on, Jester, make him laugh.
Jester I've tried, Your Majesty. I've tried. It'd be easier to make a statue laugh.
King Try again.

Reluctantly, the Jester agrees, and goes over to Prince Charming, who does not move a muscle.

Jester Your Highness—Happy Christmas ...

The Jester performs a short act. Depending on the actor's talents, this could be a funny walk, a series of funny faces, a magic trick, etc. It should be visual not verbal, and end with a funny punch or twist. But it must be short. Prince Charming doesn't react at all, even though the King and Queen, in rather forced manner, laugh and applaud. The Jester shrugs his shoulders in despair

William enters, carrying a bag or box

Prince Charming immediately springs into life

Prince Charming Any news?

The King, Queen and Jester listen intently to the following

William No, Your Highness. There's no sign of the Princess.
Prince Charming Did no-one see her coach leaving?
William No, sir, that's the extraordinary thing. At the stables they say her coach never left.
Prince Charming Then it's still there?
William Well, no. It's disappeared. Horses and footmen, too.
Prince Charming Disappeared?
William Yes. And in their place—I know it sounds silly, sir, but—

William opens the bag or box. The King, Queen and Jester come forward to look

—in their place we found these ...

The Prince pulls out the Christmas pudding. All look at each other

King A Christmas Pudding.

The Prince looks in the bag or box again

Prince Charming What on earth are those?
William Lizards, Your Highness.
Queen Lizards? (*She screams*) Aaaaah!
William And a frog.
Queen Aaaaah!
King It's all right, Ermintrude; they can't get out. Charming, what's going on?
Prince Charming I'm not sure, father. It's a mystery.
Queen What does it mean?
Prince Charming It means I'm even more determined to find the Princess. (*He looks at the glass slipper*)
William But we haven't any clues, sir.
Prince Charming Yes, we have. This. (*He holds up the slipper*). We'll scour every corner of the Kingdom till we find the girl whose foot fits this slipper. Exactly.
King (*aside*) I do believe he's perking up again.
Queen (*aside*) Yes. (*Thrilled*) Oh, go it, Charming, baby, go it!
Prince Charming And when we've found her ... (*He stops, thinks for a moment*) William, take down a Proclamation ...

SONG 14: **Spread the Word**

Prince Charming   Be it known that
                         Prince Charming
                         Will search for
                         The owner of this slipper
                         Throughout the land
                         And when he finds her
                         He'll offer her his hand.

Gasps from the others, as the music continues

Queen You mean—you'll marry her?
Prince Charming If she'll have me, yes.
Queen Charming! Baby! (*She bursts into tears*)
King Ermintrude! (*He comforts her*)
Queen I can't help it. I'm over ...
King Overtired?
Queen No. Overjoyed!
All   Spread the word
                         Spread the word
                         Have you heard?
                         Have you heard?

                         Prince Charming
                         Will search for
                         The owner of this slipper
                         Throughout the land
                         And when he finds her
                         He'll offer her his hand.

The Hairdresser, Beautician and Fairy Godmother enter, all in different guises, followed by the Children

All mingle excitedly, spreading the message
                         Spread the word
                         Spread the word
                         Have you heard?
                         Have you heard?

                         Prince Charming
                         Will search for
                         The owner of this slipper
                         Throughout the land
                         And when he finds her
                         He'll offer her his hand.

The Baron and the Ugly Sisters enter. They mingle too

                         Spread the word
                         Spread the word
                         Have you heard?
                         Have you heard?

                         Prince Charming
                         Will search for
                         The owner of this slipper
                         Throughout the land
                         And when he finds her
                         He'll offer her his hand.

                         However long it takes
                         Wherever she may be

Prince Charming   I won't give up
                          Until she marries me.

*All sing a fugue/counterpoint version of the verse, in two groups; this rises to
an exciting vocal climax*

All   Prince Charming
                          Will search for
                          The owner of this slipper
                          Throughout the land
                          (Throughout the land)
                          And when he finds her
                          He'll offer her his hand.
                          (*Shouting*) Spread the word!

Black-out

SCENE 5

The Baron's Kitchen (or hall/dining room—see Act I Scene 4)

MUSIC 14A

Cinderella carries another Christmas pudding to the table.

   The Mice enter, squeaking and excited

Cinderella Hello, Johnny and Ginnie. Happy Christmas. Close your eyes.

The Mice cover their eyes. Cinderella finds a wedge-shaped parcel

   Open! Here you are.

The Mice look at her questioningly

   It's your Christmas present.

*The Mice look pleased, and unwrap the parcel, revealing a wedge of cheese
decorated with ribbon and bow. The Mice squeak with pleasure, and kiss
Cinderella, as if to say "thank you"*

   A pleasure! It's best cheddar!

*The Mice suddenly look at each other, then back to Cinderella. They are
ashamed*

   What's the matter?

They show their empty paws

   You haven't got *me* a Christmas present? That's all right, little mice.
   There's nothing I really want—except—

The Mice squeak enquiringly

   —well, I wouldn't mind meeting the Prince again! (*Going straight on to
   stop it becoming sentimental*) Hey, do you think it's true—that he'll marry

the girl whose foot fits the slipper? (*From her apron she produces her slipper*).

The Mice nod, and point to her

No. The King and Queen would never allow it. I'm not a princess any more.

They are interrupted by the Uglies calling off

Bella ⎫ (*off, with screams of excitement*) He's coming, he's ⎰ *Speaking*
Donna ⎭ coming! (*Calling*) Cinderella! ⎱ *together*

The Mice scuttle away, carrying their present

Cinderella hides the slipper, putting it in the fireplace

Bella enters

Bella (*accusingly*) What are you doing?
Cinderella Nothing.
Bella Exactly. Nothing. You lazy lump of lethargy. Tidy up.
Cinderella I have. And I've made you another Christmas pudding.
Bella Mm. Trying to get round me, eh?
Cinderella No, I ...

Donna bursts in, dressed to kill

Donna Will I do?
Bella Will you do what?
Donna Will I do for you know who?
Bella Will you do for you know who?
Donna Yes.
Bella Who is you know who and what will you do for you know who if you *do* do?
Donna Who knows?
Bella Well, I don't. I don't know what you're talking about.
Donna The Prince. Do you think I'll attract him?
Bella Like a piece of flypaper, you mean?
Donna He's come to slip the fitter. I mean flip the sitter, sip the flitter.
Bella Fit the slipper.
Donna That's what I said.
Cinderella How exciting!
Bella As it's Christmas, as a special Christmas treat, do you want to meet the Prince?
Cinderella Oh, yes please, Bella.
Donna You really want to meet him?
Cinderella Really, Donna, please.
Bella ⎫ Aaaaah! She wants to meet the Prince! ⎰ *Speaking*
Donna ⎭ ⎱ *together*
Cinderella Yes, please.
Bella Such a shame he won't want to meet *you*.
Donna Such a shame.
Bella Into the cupboard with her.

Cinderella Oh no, please!

The Uglies frog-march her to the cupboard and lock her in

(NB: *If there is room on the set for another door, the Ugly Sisters could lock Cinderella in 'The Cellar'; this would appear to prevent her from seeing the Prince even more than locking her in a cupboard*)

Bella takes the key and puts it in her pocket or down her front.

MUSIC 14B: **Fanfare**

The Uglies, having almost been caught, move from the cupboard, titivating like mad

> *The Royal Party enters—led by the Baron. Prince Charming is followed by William, the King and Queen and the Jester. Children look in through the door and/or windows, to view the Slipper-Fitting Ceremony*

Baron Your Majesties are most welcome.

Bella ⎫
⎬ Most welcome. ⎰ *Speaking*
Donna ⎭   ⎱ *together*

The Uglies curtsy, then have to be helped up. Prince Charming nods to William, who reads formally from a scroll

William Be it known that the Prince Charming invites all eligible young ladies to try on this glass slipper.

The Jester steps forward with the slipper on a cushion

Are there any eligible young ladies in this household?

Bella There most certainly are, Billy boy!

Donna Yoo hoo!

They ogle and flutter their eyelashes

William Where are they?

Bella Where are they? What are you talking about?

Donna *Here*, dear—here.

William *You?* Eligible young ladies? You must be joking?

Bella How dare you!

Donna I'm a very legible young lady.

Bella Mm. Very legible. We can read right through you.

Donna Vicious cat!

Bella Vicious cat yourself!

Donna (*making a face at Bella*) Ughhhhh!

Bella (*making a face at Donna*) Ughhhhh!

Donna slaps Bella

Ow!

Bella slaps Donna

Donna Ow!

They kick each other

Bella } Aaaaah! { *Speaking*
Donna } { *together*

They hop about

William Ladies, please. (*He takes a chair*) You may try on the slipper.
Bella } Oh, thank you. { *Speaking*
Donna } { *together*

They both rush for the chair and crash into each other, falling over

William One at a time, please.
Bella After you, dear.
Donna After *you*, dear.
Bella No, please.
Donna I insist.
Bella } Oh, very well. { *Speaking*
Donna } { *together*

Both go for the chair and crash and fall over as before

William Ladies, *really*. Who is the youngest?
Bella } I am. { *Speaking*
Donna } { *together*
William (*in desperation, quickly, almost under his breath, pointing at each Ugly in turn*) Tinker, tailor, soldier, sailor, rich man, poor man, beggarman, thief. (*He ends up pointing to Donna*)
William (*to Donna*) Would *you* kindly sit?
Donna I'll sit as kindly as I can! (*She sits*)

The slipper is produced

SONG 15: Will the Slipper Fit?

All   Her heart goes
(*except*   Pitter patter pitter
Donna)   Will the slipper fit her?
                   Pitter patter pitter
                   Will the slipper fit?
                   See the slipper glitter
                   And she's all in a jitter
                   Will the slipper fit her
                   Or will it split?

Donna strains to squeeze her foot into the Slipper

Donna (*at last*) I've done it!

Gasps from the crowd:
     "*Impossible; I don't believe it*", etc. William investigates

William (*announcing*) Her foot is in the slipper. However—(*pulling her foot up to demonstrate*)—her heel isn't.

Laughter and catcalls from the crowd

Bella Like trying to squeeze a quart into a pint pot.
Donna (*hobbling back*) You do better. You've got feet like frying pans.

The Uglies exchange ugly looks as they swap places, Bella sits

SONG 15 (*continued*)

All	Her heart goes
(*except*	Pitter patter pitter
Bella)	Will the slipper fit her?
	Pitter patter pitter
	Will the slipper fit?
	See the slipper glitter
	And she's all in a jitter
	Will the slipper fit her
	Or will it split?

Bella reveals the glass slipper on her foot

Bella It fits! Princy, you're in luck. Take me, take me, I'm yours.
Prince Charming (*terrified*) What?

Astonishment from the Crowd

William Next summer, madam, you must come and play cricket for the
  Palace team.
Bella Eh? What for?
William We could use a third leg!

He pulls her slipper-shod shoe, revealing a false leg. All laugh.

  Sorry, madam. Out for a duck!

All quack as Bella retreats, shamefaced

Baron I apologize, Your Majesties, for my stepdaughters' behaviour. I'll
  show you out.

The King and Queen turn to leave. Prince Charming stops them

Prince Charming Wait. Surely, Baron, you have another daughter?
Baron Oh. You mean Cin ...
Bella No, he hasn't. (*She twists his arm*)
Donna Have you, Stepdaddy?
Baron Well, I ... OW!
William Oh, yes he has.
Bella } Oh, no he hasn't.   { *Speaking*
Donna }   { *together*
William (*encouraging the audience to join in*) Oh, yes he has.
Bella } Oh, no he hasn't.   { *Speaking*
Donna }   { *together*
William } Oh, yes he has.   { *Speaking*
Audience }   { *together*

Bella ⎫ **Donna** ⎭	Hasn't!	{ *Speaking* *together*
William ⎫ **Audience** ⎭	Has!	{ *Speaking* *together*

Prince Charming intervenes

Prince Charming (*to the audience*) Has the Baron another daughter?
Audience Yes.

The Uglies cower, trying to shut the audience up

Prince Charming What's her name?
Audience Cinderella.
Prince Charming Where is she?
Audience In the cupboard.
Prince Charming Where? Over here?

He lets the audience lead him to the correct door. He tries to open it. It is locked. He cannot find the key

   Where's the key?
Audience Bella's got it!

   The two Mice enter

Music. All drop back in surprise, allowing a central area in which the Mice tackle the Uglies. This is a choreographed tussle, using the fact that the Uglies hate mice. It should not take too long, but there is tension as both sides have their moments of triumph. The Mice use tactics like tickling and trying to get up the Uglies' skirts. Finally, using Bella to pinion Donna to the floor, the Mice get the key from Bella and hold it up triumphantly. Prince Charming takes the key. Dramatic drum roll. He opens the cupboard door, and leads Cinderella out towards the chair. The Uglies hobble to one side as William approaches Cinderella with the slipper

SONG 15 (*continued*)

All	Her heart goes
(*except	Pitter patter pitter
Cinderella*)	Will the slipper fit her?
	Pitter patter pitter
	Will the slipper fit?
	See the slipper glitter
	And she's all in a jitter
	Will the slipper fit her
	Or will it split?

The slipper fits perfectly

William It fits!

All cheer, except the Uglies, who faint. The Mice squeak excitedly, and kiss Cinderella

Cinderella Thank you, mice. You've given me the one Christmas present I wanted.
Prince Charming Cinderella, may I—be your Grace?
Cinderella Your Highness?
Prince Charming Will you "float with grace across the floor". Will you marry me?

The Uglies gurgle

Cinderella Yes, please, Your Highness.
Queen (*distressed*) Oh, Charming, baby, what are you doing? Throwing yourself away!
King Just stop all this nonsense at once. Her foot may fit the slipper, but you can't marry *her*. It's just not on.
Prince Charming Sorry, father. It's very much on.
King But she's a—serving girl—a . . .

The Mice interrupt him, squeaking significantly. He stops, and all watch as Johnny goes to wherever Cinderella hid the other slipper, finds it and brings it forward. Cinderella puts it on

King (*with a gasp*) She's the Princess. Ermintrude, she's the Princess!
Queen (*suddenly beaming*) Of course she is, dear. (*Going to Cinderella, arms outstretched*) Daughter!
Prince Charming We have your blessing, then?
King Of course.
Prince Charming And yours, Baron?
Baron I don't deserve such happiness, sir.

The Uglies burst into raucous tears

(*Suddenly a new man*) And you two can *shut up*. Do you hear? *SHUT UP*.

The Uglies shut up, and look aghast

For years I've put up with your selfish bullying ghastliness; for years I've allowed you to treat Cinderella like a servant, a slave in her own house; for years I've been too frightened and too stupid to speak out. But not now. From now on, I'm the boss round here. Right?

All applaud and call "bravo". The Uglies gaze at him in wonder. He looks a little embarrassed

Bella Oh, Stepdaddy.
Donna You're so—strong.
Baron And don't try to get round me. It won't wash.
William I think Bella and Donna deserve to be punished. (*To the audience*) Don't you?
Audience Yes.
Bella Mercy.
Donna Mercy.

They prostrate themselves

Bella Forgive our foolish ways.

Donna We're sorry, so sorry.

Cinderella I forgive you. (*To the others*) I think they'll behave better from now on.

Bella We will, we will.

Donna We'll join the Brownies.

Music starts as all shake hands and make friends: Cinderella and the Baron embrace

Baron I told you you had a Fairy Godmother looking after you. You didn't believe it.

Cinderella I do now. (*Closing her eyes*) Thank you, Fairy Godmother.

SONG 15A: **At the End of the Tunnel** (reprise)

Cinderella ⎫ **Baron** ⎬ (*Others* *singing* *To "AH"*)	Never lose sight Of the speck of light At the end of the tunnel It's burning bright

The Baron hands Cinderella over to Prince Charming

Cinderella ⎫ **Prince Charming** ⎬ (*Others* *Singing* *To "AH"*)	Never lose faith Never give up hope
All	At the end of the tunnel You'll be all right.

SCENE 6

The Wall of the Palace

There are snow-covered trees visible above it

Donna is discovered on a chair, painting in the last couple of words of the "Wedding Song" i.e. she is painting her own songsheet

Bella enters with all the Children

Bella Sit down, children. How are you doing, Donna?

Donna Nearly finished.

Bella Right, children. This is how it goes . . . (*She suddenly becomes aware of the audience*). Hey, Donna.

Donna (*coming down off her chair*) What?

Bella Look. Loads more children.

Donna Oh yes. So what?

Bella So why don't we ask them to join in?

Donna Go on then.

Bella comes forward

Bella Listen, children. My sister and I are so ashamed of the way we treated Cinderella, that we thought we'd arrange something really special for her wedding day today. Didn't we?
Donna We did. A wedding song. So will you all join in and sing it at the wedding?

The audience will probably agree

The Mice enter

Bella Aaaaah!

Bella jumps into Donna's arms in fright: but the Mice extend paws of friendship

Donna It's all right, Bella. They're our friends now.

All shake hands/paws

Have you come to learn the song too?

The Mice squeak

All right, you squeak it.

Bella Right, everyone. This is how it goes.

They teach the Children and the audience the song and practise it a couple of times. A competition between sections of the audience could be organized, with the Mice going into the auditorium to help

SONG 16: **Happy Wedding Day**

Audience	Let the bells ring out
(*led by*	Ding dong
the	Ding dong
Uglies)	Ding dong
	Ding dong
	Let the trumpets play
	(*Fanfare noise*)
	Good luck
	God bless you
	Happy Wedding Day.

After the last chorus, the music continues and church bells ring out

Bella Thank you, children. Quick!
Donna See you at the wedding.

All run off, as the scene changes.

SCENE 7

The Wedding/Walkdown

Joyful church bells ring out, as if the wedding ceremony has just finished

Using the Ballroom steps, the Characters enter and take their curtain calls

Finally Prince Charming and Cinderella appear and are showered with confetti

The Uglies come forward and direct a full company/audience rendering of the "Wedding Song" for the Bride and Groom

SONG 16: **Happy Wedding Day** (*continuation*)

All	Let the bells ring out
(*including*	Ding dong
the	Ding dong
Audience)	Ding dong
	Ding dong
	Let the trumpets play
	(*fanfare noise*)
	Good luck
	God bless you
	Happy Wedding Day.

The Jester steps forward

Jester Three cheers for the happy couple. Hip, hip.
All Hooray.
Jester Hip, hip.
All Hooray.
Jester Hip, hip.
All Hooray.
Jester Your Majesties, my lords, ladies and gents. The Prince and Princess will now lead the dance.

Prince Charming and Cinderella come forward. Music. We expect a formal dance, but they, and therefore everyone else, break into

SONG 16a: **The Funky Monkey** (reprise)

All   You let your arms hang down
You make a funny face
You bend your knees
And jump all over the place

Funky monkey
Funky monkey
Funky monkey
Funky monkey

Pretend you're swinging through
The branches of a tree
And you can do
The funky monkey with me.

Funky monkey
Funky monkey
Funky monkey
Funky monkey

And then you look around
To find your monkey match
And when you do
You have a jolly good scratch.

Funky monkey
Funky monkey
Funky monkey
Funky monkey
Funky monkey
Oh yeah!

CURTAIN

FURNITURE AND PROPERTY LIST

ACT I
SCENE 1

On stage: Various fairground stalls: chestnut brazier, ox-roasting, "Knock Off the Snowman's Hat", hoopla, fortune-teller's booth, large bran tub with coloured papers, streamers and book for Prince Charming
Dais
3 thrones
Small table. *On it:* scroll, tray of goblets, ornate spectacles or lorgnette, electric button connected to Christmas tree
Christmas tree

Off stage: Box of toffee apples (**Trader**)
Several masks (**Crowd**)

Personal: **William:** royal purse with coins, notebook, pencil, invitation cards
Prince Charming: ornate spectacles

SCENE 2

On stage: Kettle and iron on hob in fireplace
Ironing-board
Dresser. *On it:* pots, pans, plates, glasses, various foodstuffs and vege-tables, handbell
Kitchen table. *On it:* cloth, various foodstuffs
Chairs
Large cupboard with strong shelf. *In door:* key
Sink with practical tap
Stove. *On it:* pans
Christmas tree
In back door: key, bolt
Under sink: bucket with water, soap, scrubbing brush
Inside fireplace: shelf. *On it:* piggy bank, dish with soot
Beside fireplace: wastepaper-basket
On wall: mirror

Off stage: Basket of laundry with coloured scarf (**Cinderella**)
Scroll (**Donna**)

SCENE 3

On stage: Nil

Off stage: Sledge (**Donna, Bella, Horse**)
Carrot (**Bella**)
Ball invitations (**William**)

SCENE 4

On stage: As Scene 2
Pot with stirring spoon on stove
Plates, cutlery, food, tray with fruit bowl and cheese dish on table

Off stage: Invitation (**William**)
2 piles of Christmas-wrapped parcels (**Bella, Donna**)
Lunch tray or trolley with 3 plates of food (**Cinderella**)

SCENE 5

On stage: Christmas decorations, paperchains, etc.
Bench

Off stage: Book (**Prince Charming**)
3 invitations (**Cinderella**)

SCENE 6

On stage: Bed and bedding
Dressing-table with mirror. *On it:* various make-up articles, including
perfume spray, brushes, combs, "custard pie" face pack
2 stools
Hair drier with comedy green wig concealed in it

SCENE 7

On stage: As Scene 2
Christmas pudding on dish in oven
Pencil and paper on table
Torn invitation in wastepaper-basket
Whole invitation in wastepaper-basket

Off stage: Lizards, frog (**Cinderella**)
(Optional) Glass slippers (**Gnomes**)
Coach

Personal: **Fairy Godmother:** wand

ACT II

SCENE 1

On stage: Christmas tree with presents, *Behind it:* chair and book
Gong (optional)
Large clock
Small table
2 chairs

Off stage: Tray of pastry "goodies" (**William**)

Personal: **Jester:** staff (optional)

SCENE 3

On stage: As Act I Scene 2
            1 chair set in shadow, for Fairy Godmother
            Teacloths or handkerchiefs on table

SCENE 4

On stage: Bench
Off stage: Bag or box containing Christmas pudding, lizards, frog (**William**)
Personal: **William:** notebook, pencil

SCENE 5

On stage: As Act I Scene 2
            Christmas pudding on stove
            Wedge-shaped parcel of decorated cheese on dresser

Off stage: Scroll (**William**)
            Glass slipper on cushion (**Jester**)
            False leg (**Bella**)

SCENE 6

On stage: Chair
            Song sheet
            Painting materials

SCENE 7

On stage: Ballroom steps
Off stage: Bags of confetti (**Company**)

LIGHTING PLOT

Property fittings required: 3 sets of Christmas tree lights, various fairground stall lights, including brazier, chandelier (optional)

Various interior and exterior scenes

ACT I   Evening

To open: All lighting dim

Cue 1	**Jester:** "All the fun of the Christmas Fayre" *Snap up lighting to general effect of crisp, snowy evening, all fairground stalls lit, Christmas tree unlit*	(Page 1)
Cue 2	**King** presses button *Snap on tree lights*	(Page 3)
Cue 3	**William:** "Bella, Donna and Cinderella" *Cross-fade to special lighting for mime scene*	(Page 5)
Cue 4	At end of mime *Return to opening lighting*	(Page 6)
Cue 5	At end of Scene 1 *Cross-fade to Baron's Kitchen lighting*	(Page 8)
Cue 6	At end of Scene 2 *Cross-fade to front-cloth lighting for Scene 3*	(Page 17)
Cue 7	At end of Scene 3 *Black-out, or cross-fade to Baron's Kitchen*	(Page 23)
Cue 8	**Mice** chase **Uglies** until they collapse *Cross-fade to Palace Courtyard or Cloister*	(Page 32)
Cue 9	**Prince Charming:** "Cinderella" *Fade to Black-out, then up to Bedroom scene*	(Page 35)
Cue 10	General exit at end of Scene 6 *Cross-fade to Baron's Kitchen, night*	(Page 37)
Cue 11	**Fairy Godmother** makes magic pass at wastepaper-basket *Flash*	(Page 41)
Cue 12	**Fairy Godmother:** "Stand back"—makes pass *Flash, black-out, then return to full lighting*	(page 42)
Cue 13	**Fairy Godmother** turn off main light *Reduce lighting to conceal CINDERELLA "double"*	(Page 43)
Cue 14	**Fairy Godmother** poses at end of her song *Magical ripple effect*	(Page 43)
Cue 15	**Fairy Godmother:** "... to the Fancy Dress Ball" *Flash, black-out, then up to special transformation lighting on coach*	(Page 43)
Cue 16	**Fairy Godmother:** "... and a brand new dress" *Flash, black-out, then up to full lighting on CINDERELLA and coach*	(Page 44)

ACT II

To open: Full, glittering lighting on Ballroom

Cue 17 During Christmas waltz   (Page 53)
          Narrow lighting to spots on PRINCE CHARMING and CIN-
          DERELLA, and on clock

Cue 18 **Cinderella's** double appears   (Page 54)
          Bring up spot on her

Cue 19 After **Cinderella's** "double" exits   (Page 54)
          Bring up general lighting

Cue 20 **Prince Charming** looks at slipper   (Page 55)
          Black-out, then up to front-cloth scene

Cue 21 At end of chase sequence   (Page 56)
          Black-out, then up to Baron's Kitchen

Cue 22 **Cinderella** turns out main light   (Page 59)
          Fade to spot on CINDERELLA and MICE

Cue 23 **Cinderella** moves downstage   (Page 59)
          Fade spot, then up to Palace Courtyard or Cloister

Cue 24 At end of song: "Spread the Word"   (Page 63)
          Black-out, then up to Baron's Kitchen lighting

Cue 25 **All:** "You'll be all right"   (Page 70)
          Cross-fade to front-cloth scene, Palace Wall

Cue 26 On general exit   (Page 71)
          Cross-fade to full lighting for Finale

EFFECTS PLOT

ACT I

Cue 1	**Beautician:** "Touch your toes" (3rd time) *Loud ripping noise as BELLA stoops*	(Page 36)
Cue 2	**Bella:** "... not an all-in wrestler" *Bell rings*	(Page 36)
Cue 3	**Fairy Godmother** makes magic pass at wastepaper-basket *Puff of smoke*	(Page 41)

ACT II

Cue 4	At end of Waltz Song *First (loud) chime of midnight on clock*	(Page 53)
Cue 5	**Jester:** "It's Christmas Day" *Second chime*	(Page 53)
Cue 6	**All** say "Happy Christmas" *Third chime*	(Page 53)
Cue 7	**Cinderella** is included in celebration *Fourth chime*	(Page 53)
Cue 8	More cries of "Happy Christmas" *Fifth chime*	(Page 53)
Cue 9	**Cinderella** looks at clock *Sixth chime*	(Page 53)
Cue 10	**Cinderella** is stopped by KING and QUEEN *Seventh chime*	(Page 53)
Cue 11	**Jester:** "... a seasonal greeting" *Eighth chime*	(Page 53)
Cue 12	**Cinderella** tries to escape *Ninth chime*	(Page 54)
Cue 13	**All:** "... a Merry Christmas" *Tenth chime*	(Page 54)
Cue 14	**All:** "... a Merry Christmas" *Eleventh chime*	(Page 54)
Cue 15	**Cinderella** exits *Twelfth chime*	(Page 54)
Cue 16	**All** (singing): "Happy Wedding Day" *Church bells—continue through to Finale*	(Page 71)

Printed in Great Britain by Butler & Tanner Ltd, Frome and London